A Log of Deadwood

A Log of Deadwood

Gary David

North Atlantic Books
Berkeley, California

A Log of Deadwood

Some of these poems originally appeared in the following publications: *Black Hills Monthly Magazine, Credences, Planetary Mysteries,* and *W'Orcs.*

Cover woodcut by Dawn Senior
Cover and book design by Paula Morrison
Typeset by Patricia McGillis

North Atlantic Books
P.O. Box 12327
Berkeley, California 94701

ISBN 1–55643–156–2

Author's note: There are many Deadwoods. The primary version of this one was completed in 1983, with minor revisions being made in 1985 and 1992. As part of the concept of this logomontage, most of the sources of the various quotations have remained anonymous. My intent is not to plagiarize but to re-cognize. As Emerson somewhere said: "Every man is a borrower and a mimic. Life is theatrical and literature is a quotation."

A Log of Deadwood is sponsored by the Society for the Study of Native Arts and Sciences, a nonprofit educational corporation whose goals are to develop an educational and crosscultural perspective linking various scientific, social, and artistic fields; to nurture a holistic view of arts, sciences, humanities, and healing; and to publish and distribute literature on the relationship of mind, body, and nature.

Library of Congress Cataloging-in-Publication Data

David, Gary.
A log of deadwood / Gary David.
p. cm.
ISBN 1–55643–156–2 : $9.95
1. Wounded Knee Creek, Battle of, 1890—Poetry. 2. Dakota Indians—Wars, 1890–1891—Poetry. I. Title.
PS3554.A9148L64 1993
811'.54—dc20 93–6715
CIP

1 2 3 4 5 6 7 8 9 / 97 96 95 94 93

Acknowlegments

I would like to thank Marjorie Pontius, former head librarian of the Deadwood Public Library, Raul Ponce de Leon, Deadwood artist, and Ann Marie Baker, curator of the Adams Museum, for their assistance in researching this book. I'm also grateful to Linda Hasselstrom for the generous donation of her old PC, Ernie Grafe for sharing his computer expertise, Joe Richey for the use of his Macintosh, and Mike Forrette for his encouragement. A special thanks goes to Anita, who proof-read the manuscript, and tolerated the last days of my labor on it.

Preface

The summer of 1876 was a pivotal point in American history. Just a decade previously, the States had been welded together by the fires of civil war into one republic. Not "the United States are . . ." but "the United States *is*." The country as a whole had come into being at last, and was seen for the first time as being lasting. And yet the patriotic euphoria mounting in the months prior to the Centennial was tempered by the news in June of Custer's demise at the hands of Sioux, who were thought to have been already beaten into submission. The Gilded Age had begun.

In August of the preceding year, gold had been found "in paying quantities" on the banks of Deadwood Creek in the Black Hills of Dakota, and the rush was on. In a little over six months a few tents exploded into a city of about 10,000 greed-sparked men and women seeking instant wealth. However, the White Man refused to acknowledge that Deadwood was at the heart of the Great Sioux Reservation guaranteed in perpetuity by the Fort Laramie Treaty of 1868. The events leading up to the last Indian wars had come into play. The final curtain would fall in December of 1890, with the mass burial of over 300 Lakota (Sioux) men, women, and children wantonly slaughtered by the Army at that desolate spot on the prairie called, with sad irony, Wounded Knee.

The first known confrontation with the Amerindians was equally dramatic. One recalls Leif Eiriksson, who made the brief and ill-fated expedition to Vinland (somewhere between northern Maine and southern Labrador) c. 1000 A.D. Although he had been newly converted to Christianity, many of this period still clung to the dying pagan beliefs of the vibrant Viking Age (his father Eirik, for instance). Leif and his party encountered strange red men he called Skraelings, traded with them, and eventually fought with them. The hostility of the natives along with the harsh environment prevented him from establishing a permanent colony. Some moot theories claim an even earlier interaction between the two cultures, as far back as 2000 B.C. These theories are supported by a recent discovery of pre-runic petroglyphs and remnants of copper mining north of Lake Superior.* It is thought that some of these ancient Norsemen even penetrated into

---

*Barry Fell, *Bronze Age America,* Little, Brown & Co., Boston, 1982.

the interior of the continent. At any rate, Odin (the Norse god of war, poetry, and magic) once walked the red shores of America. His legacy was carried on, generation after generation, through the bloodlines of those who, for the most part, came to settle the heartland—i.e. those of Scandinavian and German descent.

By the middle of the nineteenth century, it seemed the country was wide open and there for the taking. The Oregon Trail, the gold rushes in California, Colorado, and Montana, various military expeditions and the building of forts, the series of broken treaties with the tribes, the Homestead Act—all these whittled away at the lands and power of the Indian. By 1876 America's future looked the brightest—its possibilities had reached their highest point in the sky. The nation's summer solstice had come, and the fall of the sun had begun. Dotted with medicine wheels and runic megaliths, the High Plains waited. Across that span of sun-scorched land known as the Great American Desert, the days grew shorter. Under the Bridge of a thousand years joining memories of the old country with dreams of future prosperity, lengthening shadows gathered.

Just five years before the Centennial, the maligned and beloved poet Walt Whitman published his "Passage To India." He fervently believed America was the vital link between Old World Europe and Hindu Asia: Europe with its broken castles of chivalry, its grotesquely gothic cathedrals, its history of oppressive feudalism, and its dead languages; Asia with its fabled temples and ruins, its Vedic texts, its mystifying rituals and customs, and its sacred wisdom of silence. Whitman saw the Manifest Destiny of the westward movement across North America as simply a means—the means to spiritually circumnavigate the globe, a way to make the holy circle (the "rondure") of the Earth complete. After the laborer, the engineer, the scientist, and the entrepreneur had done their work, only then would come the poet, the "true son of God." Through the seeds of his living word, humankind and the Earth would fuse in mystical union. Thus the poet would be the real redeemer of that state of grace the primitive races once had known. Any lesser realization of this dream would indicate America's failure to fulfill its great spiritual potential, and thereby signify the triumph of crass materialism. What faith in the modern!

In the same year the sun began to darken over the skies of Europe. Arthur Rimbaud had written "Le Bateau ivre" ("The Drunken Boat"). The poem was his sea, fraught with dangerous deliriums and ineffable ecstasies. He created an alchemy of the word. He tried to become the quintessential magician of mirage, the denizen of dreamscape, the lotos-eater of language. He soon would stridently and bitterly declare his bad blood, the rapacious ways of his self-proclaimed inferior race—the Norse and the Gauls with their gluttonous hankering after God. He tried to escape into the opiate wonders of the Orient, the archetypal Eden, or the heaven of hashish, only to awaken dazed and vomit-stained from a nightmare of hell. He had entered into the Bardo realm of the Tibetan Book of the Dead, with its alternate visions of resplendent beauty and awe-inspiring terror: all illusion, all maya, all hopelessness. He concluded with despair and exhaustion that the battle for one soul is as brutal as all the battles of men. At age twenty this *enfant terrible* and instinctive poetical genius gave up his art completely, only to become a slave-trader and gun-runner in Abyssinia. He never returned to poetry. Through years of silence until his death at age thirty-seven, the ghosts of Rimbaud's self-indicted race were dealing doom-drugs to his own bizarre past.

These ancestral ghosts still haunt the shores of America. (Poe, Melville, and Hawthorne were the first here to flesh them out.) They are wandering ghosts who have no place on the Earth's great circle to go. Thirsty ghosts who drink deeply from the blood-pit of memory. Ghosts who slosh aimlessly through the myth-bog of nightmare. Ghosts who move with the body of the Aurora Borealis. Plundering ghosts with Viking names. Ghosts exiled from the state of Nature who lust after salvation like a beast in rut. Ghosts who live by the sword, the gun, the H-bomb. The Nordic Twilight of the Gods is fated to be played out within each one of these wayward souls lost upon the Plain of Death. Rudderless upon the inland ocean, they drift at the center of a nation that practices systematic genocide in the name of Progress, Science, Reason—all capitalized, all G.N.P., all material gains and losses. Personal tragedy takes on epic proportions. The fiction of history and the reality of mythos merge. Facts become incontestably subjective as Nature's law breaks down into an anarchy of multitudinous desires. Each life is a Bardo state between lives, torn by the winds of karma and incessant change. Midway in our lifespan is a place we have come to, as if awakening from a deep sleep. Midway between Europe and Asia is America. At the center of America is an island of evergreen the Lakota call Paha Sapa, the sacred Black Hills, the heart of the world. It is a place burning in time. It is *A Log of Deadwood*.

Prelude

The United States—bounded on the north by the Aurora Borealis, on the south by the precession of the equinoxes, on the east by primeval chaos, and on the west by the day of Judgement.

—John Fiske, *Bounding the United States*

"A forested island in a grassland sea" is a descriptive phrase that graphically portrays the Black Hills.

—Sven G. Froiland, *Natural History of the Black Hills*

. . . the basic idea of bardo: "bar" means in between, and "do" means island or mark; a sort of landmark which stands between two things. It is rather like an island in the midst of a lake.

—Chögyam Trungpa,
Commentary to *The Tibetan Book of the Dead*

I looked now upon the world as a thing remote, which I had nothing to do with, no expectations from, and indeed no desires about: in a word, I had nothing indeed to do with it, nor was ever like to have; so I thought it looked as we may perhaps look upon it hereafter, viz. as a place I had lived in, but was come out of it; and well might I say, as Father Abraham to Dives, *Between me and thee is a great gulph fix'd.*

—Daniel Defoe, *Robinson Crusoe*

This is a kind of charm
A circle dance
dreamt from a place
where pine lingers
continually on the air
the moon is always full
and fires soar with spirits
clothed in the body of dark
moving into silhouettes of light.

—Judy Platz

"But it is a long way to the Emerald City, and it will take you many days. The country here is rich and pleasant, but you must pass through rough and dangerous places before you reach the end of your journey." . . . they came to a big building, exactly in the middle of the City, which was the Palace of Oz, the Great Wizard. ". . . my people have worn green glasses on their eyes so long that most of them think it really is an Emerald City, and it certainly is a beautiful place, abounding in jewels and precious metals, and every good thing that is needed to make one happy."

—L. Frank Baum, *The Wonderful Wizard of Oz*

A mandala as construct, as architecture, is center of city/is bound to the city/binds the city to the world by transformation of chaos into an ordered cosmos. It is man mirrored. It is the chaos of man,

"sea
sky
ceiling
floor
city's
pane"

(I, 5) in a world of particulars.

—Earel Neikirk on *The Mandala Book* by Tom Beckett

The mandala as used in ceremonials are of great significance because their centres usually contain one of the highest religious figures: either Shiva himself—often in the embrace of Shakti—or the Buddha, Amitaba, Avalokiteshvara, or one of the great Mahayana teachers, or simply the *dorje*, symbol of all the divine forces together, whether creative or destructive. The text of the *Golden Flower*, a product of Taoist syncretism, specifies in addition certain 'alchemical' properties of this centre after the manner of the *lapis* and the *elixir vitae* . . .

—C.G. Jung, *Psychology and Alchemy*

The correspondence of Odin and Varuna is striking. Both are fundamentally magicians. To be sure, Nordic magic presents its own characteristics for which it would be vain to seek equivalents in India. But the gift of shape-shifting so characteristic of the former coincides with the *maya* that the latter employs so abundantly. . . . The heroes killed in battle belong to Odin and continue in Valhalla a life of unending feasts and duels which are no more than sport, and this happy destiny is extended to anyone else who marks himself with the sign of Odin before death. Just so we have seen the Indian funeral ritual promise the Aryan dead—all the Aryan dead, it would seem—as the end of their journey the residence where they will see the two kings Varuna and Yama [Lord of Death], while "tasting pleasure at their will."

—Georges Dumézil, *Gods of the Ancient Northmen*

. . . the sense of what is real, the thought if after all it should
prove unreal.
The doubts of the day-time and doubts of the night-time, the
curious whether and how,
Whether that which appears so is so, or is it all flashes and
specks?
Men and women crowding fast in the streets, if they are not
flashes and specks what are they?

—Walt Whitman

. . . heroes, heroines, celestial warriors, and the faith-protecting deities, male and female, each bedecked with the six bone-ornaments, having drums and thigh-bone trumpets, skull-timbrels, banners of gigantic human hides, human-hide canopies, human-hide bannerettes, fumes of human-fat incense, and innumerable kinds of musical instruments, filling [with music] the whole world-systems and causing them to vibrate, to quake and tremble with sounds so mighty as to daze one's brain, and dancing various measures, will come to receive the faithful and punish the unfaithful.

—from Day Seven of *The Tibetan Book of the Dead*
(compiled and edited by W.Y. Evans-Wentz)

Well, by and by the king gets up and comes forward a little, and works himself up and slobbers out a speech, all full of tears and flapdoodle, about it's being a sore trial for him and his poor brother to lose the diseased, and to miss seeing the diseased alive after the long journey of four thousand mile, but it's a trial that's sweetened and sanctified to us by this dear sympathy and these holy tears, and so he thanks them out of his heart and out of his brother's heart, because out of their mouths they can't, words being too weak and cold, and all that kind of rot and slush, till it was just sickening; and then he blubbers out a pious goody-goody Amen, and turns himself loose and goes to crying fit to bust. And the minute the words were out of his mouth somebody over in the crowd struck up the doxologer and everybody joined in with all their might, and it just warmed you up and made you feel as good as church letting out. Music *is* a good thing; and after all that soul-butter and hogwash I never see it freshen up things so, and sound so honest and bully.

—Mark Twain, *The Adventures of Huckleberry Finn*

Deadwood, like every other big mining town that has yet been located in the West, was full of rough characters, cut-throats, gamblers and the devil's agents generally. Night and day the wild orgies of depraved humanity continued; a fiddler was an important personage, provided he would hire out to saw all night in a saloon, and the concert singer was a bonanza, especially if the voice were clothed in petticoats. The arbiter of all disputes was either a knife or a pistol, and the graveyard soon started with a steady run of victims. Sodom and Gomorrah were both dull, stupid towns compared with Deadwood, for in a square contest for the honors of moral depravity the Black Hills' capital could give the people of the Dead Sea cities three points in the game and then skunk them both.

—J.W. Buel, *Heroes of the Plains*

Nous savons donner notre vie tout entière tous les jours.
(We know how to give our whole life every day.)

—Arthur Rimbaud
(translated by Louise Varèse)

. . . for the Sioux believe that these are the days at the end of the world when the moon will turn red and the sun will turn blue. But since for the traditional man everything in the macrocosm has its counterpoint in the microcosm, there may also be an end of the world for the individual here and now, whenever he receives illuminations or wisdom from *Wakan Tanka*, so that his ego or ignorance dies, and he then lives continually in the Spirit.

—Joseph Epes Brown, *The Sacred Pipe*

The sun turns black,   earth sinks into the sea,
The hot stars down   from heaven are whirled;
Fierce grows the steam   and life-feeding flame,
Till fire leaps high   above heaven itself.

—"Voluspa" (from *The Poetic Edda*)

About 2000 years ago the Nordic Teutons began to emerge from their homes in the frozen north. Toward the east, south and west they moved slowly but resolutely, overrunning the old Roman Empire, displacing and exterminating entire races. In England they left hardly a vestige of the former inhabitants. They continued expansion against the laws of God and man, penetrating Asia, Africa, Australia and America, and here in 1876 we observe them beginning to filter through into the seemingly inaccessible fastnesses of the Black Hills. But they carried on the tradition of their ancestors, aggressive and arrogant, with a haughty contempt for other peoples. "Blessed are the meek for they shall inherit the earth." On hearing this an Englishman, a true representative of the Nordic Teutons, exclaimed, "Then we are the meek." The invasion of the Hills was but a small wave of the general conquest on the earth by the blond Nordics.

—Henry Onsgard, *South Dakota Historical Collections,* Vol.XIII

Then a weird ruck of foot and horse,
Buckskin and mail and worn homespun,
Crossbow, javelin, flintlock gun,
Breeds and creeds of ages mixed—
Steel crusader and Viking Norse,
Priest and Puritan, Gaul and Hun,
But, savage or gentle, swart or blond,
The ghosts all marched with their dim eyes fixed
On the pass that would show them the country beyond.

—Badger Clark

Prolog

Out of Ginnunga Gap
the first matter: the chaos
of rock & darkness, gas
& dust, ice & fire, stars
of the farthest galaxies, comets,
asteroids & planets—all
whirl & fall in the abyss
of nothingness. Day upon light-year
day warped upon blind points
in space like pearls formed round
grains of sand, *they*

enter the sacred circle, come
(in order) to be its center.
An empty ocean blue as Odin's eye
flows from the heart
of the oldest giant beneath
an equally empty sky.
Without clouds, without waves. Still
as the whole world holding
its breath, the land stretches out
the length of the fallen giant.
From under its salty armpit
the first man & woman are sweat.
In the air of spruce & aspen
to the north, its feet
beget the race of frost giants.
Its matted hair bristling red
cedar & prickly pear in the south
crowns a mammoth head
with fire. Its tears become
hot springs, its spirit steam. Its granite
backbone thrusts up
a range of mountains gray
as grandfathers. Across the sky-dome
of its skull, the moon full
of quicksilver heads home.

The sulphur sun rises &
runs for its life. Upon the horizon
the eyeteeth of the mythic wolf
gleam. The most archaic site
on this wild continent, the pure heart
of the New World is soon transfused
with the old country's blood.
This sacred circle
                    is a crucible
of gold. An inland island
of evergreen: the Indians call it
Paha Sapa. A rich sap runs, ever
thick, ever old. "Ah! . . . Ah! . . ."
the grasses of the plains seem
to whisper, their waves breaking ashore.
Come, come into the Black Hills. Dream
petrified birds, putrefied songs, Deadwood
of Dacotah Territory or
the New World Tree. Drop
a round white stone within
the still waters of time. It echoes all
Deadwood's annular rings. Like Odin's
golden band they call
Draupnir (the "Dropper"), the sun
makes many diurnal rings
out of the one (fire). Out of the deep
blue day after day
                    resounds
                              across this land
their new-found fate. *They*
have not heard
a sound
at the center. They are
out
upon the plain plowing
a circle
in the brain. They are
the days
of their lives lost
between lives between

dead or alive.
Wanted, there is
no place they are
safe to hide
in. The inner membrane
of the giant's skull
is the cloudless sky's
blue hide
-out. They are
there to hide their
faces. Upon the face
of the still water's
mirror, the first
Clear Light will stare
them down. Merely
an illusion, the sea
sees the worst
that can happen.
"Seize the day!"
they say. Really
they are dry &
they are you. You
((A(U)M)) is
at the center. Yet
you have not heard
the Book of the Dead
Wood sound
out. They are
this Clear
Light. You are
unclear
as to where
they will go.
Wanting but unwanted
as a rabid dog
wandering
the D.T., they are
thirsty
after what (?)
imaginary number

of log days. They are
delirious
with untolled lives or one
blink
out of the blue
eye. All
the same
they arrive
(what they think is)
alive. You see them
thru
their own eyes
at sundown up
the cañon leading into
Deadwood. The first
of the 49 days
at the center
burns
like the Aurora
Borealis or
the first matter
thirsting after
the everlasting. GOLD
IN THE GRASSROOTS!
the news
headlines say.
They will
be you & me. Still
we have not heard
what's already been
said
all our lives: dead
word.

Day 1 **Wednesday, June 21, 1876—password:** ***ignorance***

In-bourne on the back of the eight-leggéd horse
White Breath toward Deadwood
of Dacotah Territory,
Farley O'Din
then rode down the gulch as the sun
rested on the western rimrock
a moment, & was gone. Its journey
north to this day is done. Come down
on this ramshackle goldbust town, the weight
of a hundred summers of black iron lie
in the red, hot dust.
The fate of this man: the same
as the fate of this land. Mystickally
both in the balance
hang.

From the Central Realm, called the Spreading Forth
of the Seed, the first peaceful deity, white
in color, seated upon a lion-throne [mountain], bearing
an eight-spoked wheel in his hand, embracing
the Mother of the Space of Heaven . . .
hovers
over the granite cañon. From his heart
nothing
but a blue light
blinding!
Out front
the Old Style Saloon, O'Din unaware
tethers his mist-shaded mare, takes off
his broad-brimmed hat her shadow feathers, mops
his brow, stops to cast (with the wyrd
of a blood-dripped rune) his good eye right
at the heart of the night &
the Big Dipper pours out
the Aurora Borealis: a dull white light.
Campfires flicker up & down
the gulch. Buffeted back & forth
by a rising north wind, the howl

of a timber wolf (really one
Smokey Jones playing taps) echoes ethereally
the glow of the embers' dying sun.
The 'spectors' lids grow heavy.
Some are already dead
to the world. From the Celestials'
joss house in the "badlands"
on lower Main St., a whiff of sandlewood
incense in the wind mingles
with a bitter-sweet minor
melody from the bar:

> "Fire on the mountain, lightnin' in the air,
> Gold in them hills, an' it's waitin' for me there."

O'Din heads inside for an amber shot
of redeye. He sees a *Pioneer* laid out
on a table. In faded El Dorado style ("a shade
between the Aurora Borealis and
a new $13 saddle"), the news
shimmer on the paper:

> "Let the noble white man have this country
> rich in silver and gold, a delightful
> climate, and whose valleys are covered
> with luxuriant grass, beautiful beyond
> description, and whose lofty mountains
> tower far beyond the thunder's home."

To the pine-clad north, the shadows
of the white spirits dance
away the night of the first day
as dreadnaught O'Din's gut rumbles
& reels with the drunken blood
wayward Deadwood burns with.

Day 2 **Thursday, June 22, 1876—password:** ***hatred***

From the Eastern Realm, over the deep
blue sea shines
a white light: a boat-load
of goods, sales, the World
Serpent
          sunk. Though Thorvald Bloodaxe thunders
over the water, still, the waves
of molten glass into the heart turn
to buffalo grass in his dream's wake.
Over the dry plain his Conestoga wagon
wheels toward Deadwood—the counter-spin
illusion of spokes spoken
for. *Forward Ho!* & no
turning back. Here the new nation
                                        hears
Teutonic blood that laps its shores
inland. Loud as a thousand thunderclaps taking
the land of the war-loving Sioux
Indian by storm, a din
of immigrants crowds the wharves
to the heartland's forts. The manifest destiny
of the White Man imports
the old sin: a gallimaufry of time
pieces & gilt-framed mirrors, blunderlust
whiskey & poxed blankets, barbed
wire & wind mills, revolving
fire irons all turning
out a Viking-like hatred
for anyone at home
with their own land. Simple as dirt
yet fathomless beyond
measure, the treasure trove
of roving Norse myths hoarded
in the heart's given
luster to love upon this basin:
bloodshed & dearth. Dip down the cup
to memories of the deep. Drink

to underground dwarfs: smiths pounding
a faint sound working
its way into consciousness, working
metals into weapons, pounding
hammers thru dull blue smoke
& brimstone flame finding
its way toward light, waking
to a new foundry
                                        of the brain. The idea
                                                            (the ideal
progress): the "civilized world" marches
its martial strain (virile
& comely) on the eardrums
of Wayland Weston Smith (the preacher's brother)
hacking next to Bloodaxe
in the wagon headed straight
for Deadwood. At dusk
upon the horizon the Black Hills hover
like a blue mirage: a homesteader's castle, a casket
filled with gold dust, the ungodly mills
of some tightwad corporate "angel"—whatever
one desires
                              appears
as the white light of the second day
                                                                      fades away.

Day 3 **Friday, June 23, 1876—password:** ***vanity***

From the Realm down in the South, land
of fire free for all &
hot chili peppers not
for the yellow-bellied, under
the blaze of an unblinking sun, the earthy
Lucky L. Coyote

along with his sidekick compañero
Ink Tommy the Spider came to play
a trick or two on a score or more
of saloons that shot up (redeyed)
overnight in Deadwood. Tommy marks
the cards as Lucky's sleight
of hand baffles the rabble
of aurific placer rushers. From the first
those poor suckers were dead-panned
for all the hard-won gold dust
their bullbags would hold. At the end
of the bar this cunning sharp works
his cards to a furious blur. Hearts
come up diamonds, clubs
spades as the joker shuffles
like a minstrel among the white-faced

poker pack. Unlike Hickok, Lucky's back
never faced the door. Still he strutly
met his match in the butt
of some whore, who burned his ass
with the same box she poxed
his cock. The morning after
swapping spit & more
with this tart, his whopping member oozed
oodles of dull yellow pus. Bruised
& house-broken, his ego smelled
trouble. Her double-trick had turned
bigger headed Lucky sour
on the fairer sex, & for some time
sore.

Day 4 **Saturday, June 24, 1876—password:** ***desire***

From the Western Realm, the fire
of the land spreads
her cock-hunting thighs
across the back of a stud
& rides the Cheyenne Trail
toward Deadwood. A dull red dust
like the wanderlust thirst
of disembodied spirits whirls
in tiny twisters over the plain.
A hail of arrows
grazes her rainbow bows
& pricks the way
this whore's horse's nose
goes—straight
down on the rising man
in the moon. Setting
the horizon on fire,
Freya Freeley blows
a cheerful tune. She knows
the terror of the red
-gold tears as well
as the hungry wonders
of the silver apples
to come. A series
of old blunders blind
& white as the year's
first blizzard is
soon undone
in the sweaty arms
of summer.

"Riding boy from Powder River,
Rides the broncs until they shiver,
Rides the girls until they quiver,
He's the riding boy!"

Day 5 **Sunday, June 25, 1876—password:** ***greed***

From the Northern Realm, the frost giants come
firm & clean as the hoary winds
thru the evergreen that root
round the rune-echoing well
                                        of Dr. Mimer. Dr. Mimer sees
right thru these Hel-sounding fellows
the firmament mirrored within
a window of ice forming
a dull green light. He goes for it:
a green olive bobbing
in a double shot of redeye. A god's eye
colliding colors, the kaleidoscope
of the end of the Milky Way with
the Aurora Borealis starts this day
to bleed together. Its reflection
in the well of the heart's weather (the future
up in the air) forms
the only picture of the wisdom
                                        of perfected action
                                here
on earth. Mimer is head doctor
of Deadwood. Everybody consults it
like a mystick almanack.

> "An ague very violent; the fit
> held me seven hours, cold
> fit and hot, with faint
> sweats after it."

Still they all mistake the line
in the newspaper the day before
for eternal designs—a sign of the ill
feelings the hereafter has
for the here-&-now:

> "We made the open country
> through a park of oak and timber, so

picturesque, so beautiful, that
the dullest soul would have been
lifted into a higher life." Or

his low-down on Yellow Hair's paramount
lack of horse sense:

"By the red-willowed banks
of the Greasy Grass I see
(more than a day's jaunt
from here) there
ain't no body 't all left
to doctor." Doctor
Mimer remarks absent
-mindedly to himself at the meat
market counter—a pound of ground
bear on the scales, a Sunday afternoon
in the balance, the full moon
rising red, but on the run.

Day 6 **Monday, June 26, 1876**

From the 4 divisions of the heart (together
with its center making
5 directions in all):

the dull white light of the gods
    of consciousness
the dull blue light of the wild beasts
    of matter
the dull yellow light of the human beings
    of feelings
the dull red light of the hungry ghosts
    of perceptions
the dull green light of the frost giants
    of conceptions—

all the illusory lights
of the Borealis pouring over the cañon's rimrock mingle
with the gray smoke of the 'spectors' campfires. It seems
a scene out of some body's distant memory. Dreams
of the day's luster (the 2300 dollar take
out of the #6 below Discovery) stake
out their territory. Out of dull dust the figures
astronomically rise:

Farley O'Din &Wild Bill,
Thorvald Bloodaxe, Lucky L. Coyote, Freya Freeley, & Dr. Mimer;
Sheriff Tyrane & Lord of Death,
Wayland Smith, Calamity Jane, Coolee Q., & Preacher Smith,
Corporal White & a Hel-host of others—
Charley Utter & Johnny Slaughter,
Brick Pomeroy & Brant Street,
Bloody Dick Seymour & Banjo Dick Brown,
Slippery Sam & Bummer Dan Baum,
M.C. Thum & Moses Manuel,
Boone May & Madam Mustachio,
E.B. Farnum & Major Vroom,
Swill Barrel Jimmy & Coal Oil Johnny,
Cocaine Annie & Poker Alice Tubbs,
Homestake Harry & Nutshell Will,

Nuckles Dan & Kitty Leroy,
                    Socks Cloud & Club Foot Frank,
Nat Love & Norman Storms,
                    Inez Sexton & Al Swearengen,
Seth Bullock & Sol Star,
                  Crook Nosed Jack & Big Nosed George,
Frenchy Cachlin & Billy the Oyster—
                         all of 'em, gather, a heap
outside the Bella Union Theater:
'spectors en masse moving
south down Main St. mirror
the spirit path of the Milky Way.
The pavement: fool's (fake) gold.
The payment: the dead heat
the heart's migrations
                  make.

DRAMATIS PERSONAE MANDALA AND MAP

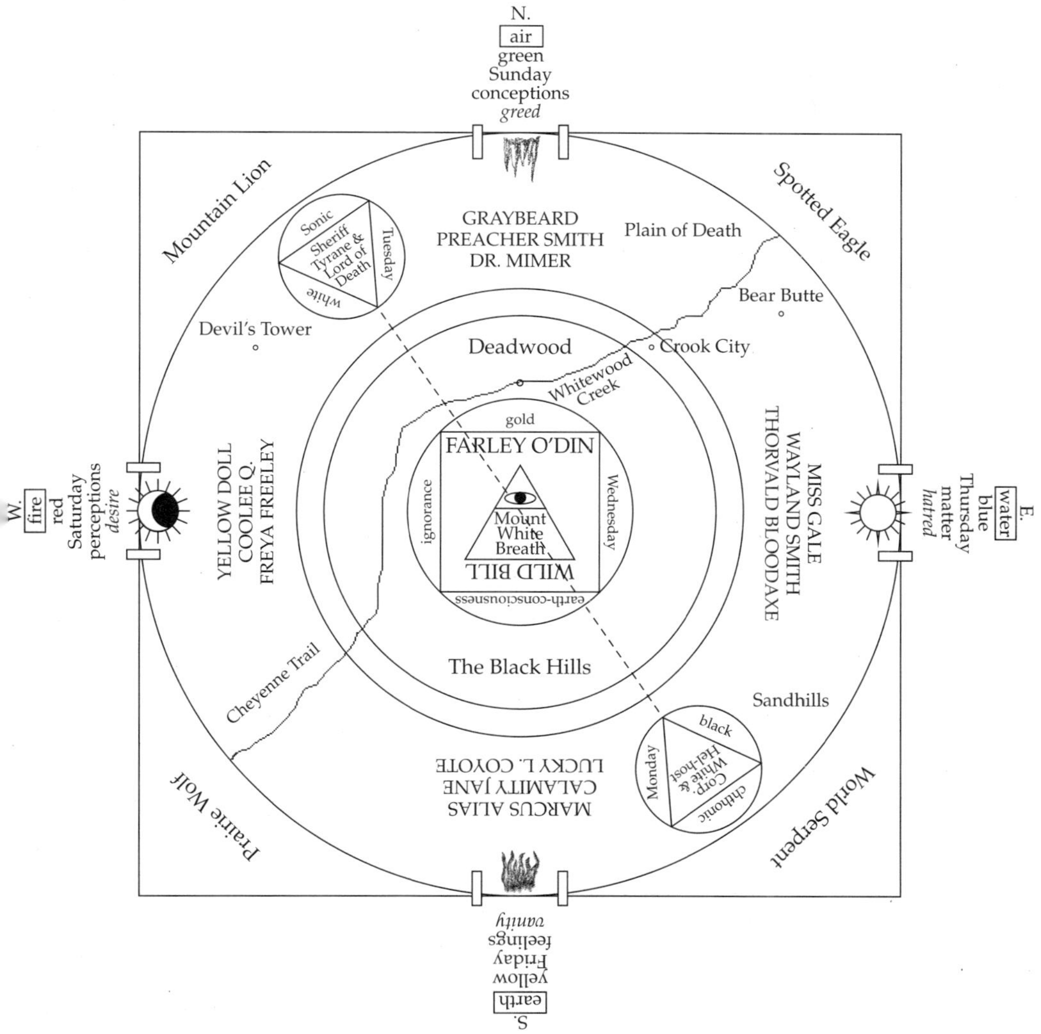

-----Dotted line represents the vertical axis of the New World Tree

Day 7 **Tuesday, June 27, 1876** (A way to read this day: slowly down the left side of the page, then back to the beginning, reading alternate sides of the page, left to right, line by line.)

from the throat the knowledge	leaves
holds	(leaf)
weight	leave
a thousand times	(light)
a thousand thunders	the breath
words	
resound	here
around	of Death
	from the mouth
the New World Tree	thereby released
Dead Wood	be
cross cut	
saw	chord would
mandala	present
rings	this one
	lives
song	past
numbers	from many
over	karmic parts
4	inherit

billion
years
old Lord of
Dance
hears
the constant
hum
within
the pith
chants
within
the bark
echo

the bars
gold
bullion
measures
the thirst
thrust
upward on
the path
heavy

hearts

heavy
the path
upward on
thrust
the thirst
measures
bullion
gold
the bars

echo
the bark
within
chants
the pith
within
hum
the constant
hears
Dance
old Lord of
years

hearts
inherit
karmic parts
from many
past
lives
this one
present
chord would

be
thereby released
from the mouth
of Death
here

the breath
(light)
leave
(leaf)
leaves

billion
4
over
numbers
song

rings
mandala
saw
cross cut
Dead Wood
the New World Tree

around
resound
words
a thousand thunders
a thousand times
weight
holds
from the throat the knowledge

Day 8 **Wednesday, June 28, 1876**

From the headwaters on down
the banks of False Bottom Creek, all the 'spectors
expect color at every dip to flash
flood their pans. Instead the dreary green
birch & aspen leaves flutter
whispers in the wind of the rich
gold still a dry season away. Mirrored in the ear
the cold creek mutters its utter indifference
to any song of sacrifice a 'spector might make
of his son. High atop Mt. Moriah (one day known
as Boothill) O'Din surveys the terrain
of Deadwood:

> *. . . with three heads, six hands, and four feet . . .*
> *the right head white, the left red, the middle*
> *dark-brown, the body radiating flames, the nine*
> *eyes widely gaping in terrifying gaze, the eyebrows*
> *quivering like lightning, the teeth protruding*
> *and overlapping, the mouth giving out piercing*
> *whistling sounds . . .*

Shine St. Sherman St. Lee St. Main St. Pine St. Wall St. Gold St.
(even the other-worldly Chinatown) all resound with
pounding hammers, rasping saws, cracking whips, cursing bull
-whackers, braying mules, mooing cattle. . .

> *His heads are adorned with skulls and symbols*
> *of sun and moon. He wears a garland*
> *of black snakes strung with human heads.*
> *His first right hand holds a wheel,*
> *the second a sword, the third a battle-ax.*
> *His first left hand holds a bell,*
> *the second a skull, the third a plow.*

Farley crosses his eyes: the moon eclipses
the sun. Now from afar he sees
himself

as Deadwood: one vast beast
in rut.

"... a dense, dark mass of surging, pushing, struggling
male humanity, every business place open and traffic
in full blast." [as Annie Tallent, first historian
of the Black Hills knew it.]

Into the wilderness this wildebeest rushes
after a pair of hindquarters: the flesh
which leads to the motherlode
its quicksilver seed.

... her right arm around his neck, her left hand
holding a blood-filled red shell to his mouth.
The shell makes a crackling thunderous sound.
Both bodies radiate brightly, each with a flaming
scepter.

Into the Tree at the center
of the great hall of the world
where one day he'll hang
9 nights to learn rune-lore, O'Din plunges
his wrathful sword of thought
up to the hilt: into the blood
of the lingworm staining the arm
up to the shoulder, into the dead
wood of every broken back
history book, into Volsunga Saga
& songs of the Edda, into the pulp
of dime novels & headline
news, into blues & rock, flood
& fire, into the ash smoldering
into every sweaty pore
& smutty gash, into every body
of blonde maidens gathering
the fallen from old war-flames, into
every time
& place
& none

may unlock
his blade
(his blood)
from the door of
immortality.

The goldbugs who dug
their living out of Deadwood
say: Why not
make hay while the sun . . .
runs its course. It's the curse
the 'spectors share
with the sparrow: it has to fly
thru the great hall, in one door
& out the other, out
to fly with icy wings
of the ever-blasting blizzard. For good
or bad, their bones are warm
such a brief span. On the other hand
(leaf by leaf) a book of gold sleeps
for ages in the earth. It waits
for the sun's all-knowing eye to hover
over the mirror of its pages.

Day 9 Thursday, June 29, 1876

Thorvald Bloodaxe & Wayland Smith were
(from the eastern quarter of the brain)
walking down manure-inured Main talking
of industry, the two
senses of the word—a turd
every step of the way.

THORVALD: It's jist plain hard work.
Sweat o' th' brow. Bust
yer balls, that's all.

WAYLAND: Oh no, it's much more. I see
great cities of iron linking
the land from sea to sea.
Rail and telegraph lines will shine
the light of civilization down on
this savage country heretofore blinded
by superstition and barbaric heresies.

THORVALD: Nah! Yer on yer own here.
Stake out yer homestead. Stoke
th' fire good. Make all th' thunder
yer Winchester kin muster.

Back & forth they go
that way: this
incessant sidestepping
the real matter at hand or
wanting
to take the land but
leave the crap, underhandedly
understanding
nothing of the warrior's creed
of sacrifice & death:
a necessity to feed
the ravines with blood—
good red blood
shed like water

to make the land
green again. Meanwhile
a half a realm away
Judge Kidder in the House
of Representatives:
"The time has arrived
when people are not to be deceived
by well-rounded sentences, poetical
effusions, or charming fictions.
Desolated homes, thousands
of widows and orphans cry out
that these murderers must leave
these lands to the quiet possession
of those who are able and willing
to assist the earth in giving
forth its increase . . ."

—arguing the extinction
of the Fort Laramie Treaty
of 1868, which ceded all lands
from the Missouri west
to the Shining Mountains
to the Sioux Nation: their
inalienable reservation.

Day 10 **Friday, June 30, 1876**

On her day Freya freely
gives it away. It
becomes him (Coyote), his cod
fry & pussyfish filet. His sole
refrain:
"The whole

she

-bang!"
(from the southern quarter of the brain)
he catholically sang
day in & day out.
Lucky pathetically remarks
to his card-marking pard
Ink Tommy, man to man &
dog to bug:

"I'm going so nuts
over this chick
my milk cow
won't come!"

Down the porked barrel
of Madam Freeley's relay
in the body politic, she licks
with a quick flick
all *obiter dicta.*

Day 11 Saturday, July 1, 1876

Drunk & barefoot up
to her ears, Freeley dances
on the balcony of the female
seminary they call
the Gem. All her boys
gather round, roll up
dollar bills, put one end in
their mouths, the other down
her mound. Currency mingling with
cunnilingus, she lights up
to take a drag. Her lips (fast
-toking the legal tender
like a Bull Durham) at last break
into a prick-eating grin.

Broad backs & shoulders sweaty
with six days hard labor ache
come Saturday night
to go down on some
(soft) thing.

"One night of love don't make up
fer six nights alone;
But I'd rather have one than none
'cause I'm flesh 'n' bone." sung throaty

Freya deep to one such well
-hung newcomer. "All
men got soft spots where. . .

(from the western quarter of the brain)

they make love alike."
She swallows hard on
each head: an ocean
of semen swelling her belly
the way the heart does
blood.

"Dreamin' of home wherever I roam.
I'm dreamin' of home and of mother."

"Captain Jack left for Omaha last Wednesday
taking with him a large assortment
of specimens and the good wishes
of all the boys."

Day 12 Sunday, July 2, 1876

"I will lift up mine eyes unto the hills, from whence cometh
my help." Henry Weston Smith, minister, sawyer, miner, poet.

(From the northern quarter of the brain) just 49 days &
this Gold St. godspeller will wonder the road to Crook City:

. . . was it I? . . . was it I? . . . was it I? . . . was it I? —who
left his Connecticut congregation & a wife & kids in Kentucky

& his life along that Black Hills defile, his light shot out
past the blood-blotted notes for a sermon, past the Bible

in his hands (that wordly comfort), past the last glimpse
of empty sky, the last warble of a bird, the last scent

of grass & granite at his back—his path of light from
earth into water into air into fire into ether, awareness

past preaching about, a candle buried in the sun, a Clear Light
his past reflected (on the glass) darkly, years after he's gone

the way: the shade of a mountain lion feels the moon
of blood rise from his black *Book of the Seven Seals.*

"And the heavens departed as a scroll when it is rolled
together; and every mountain and island were moved . . ."

Day 13 Monday, July 3, 1876

A white death goddess from the east holds a corpse in the right hand like a club, a blood-filled skull in her left. A yellow death goddess comes from the south, with bow and arrow, ready to shoot.

> ". . . at least a dozen Indians ran at me out of the brush, and you bet I ran and hollered for help. In a minute more, two or three of them shot at me."

> > The sacrifice is of this nature: of everything that is male they offer nine heads . . .

A red death goddess from the west bears a banner depicting a crocodile. A black death goddess from the north carries a scepter in one hand, a blood-filled skull in the other.

> "I felt a sharp, stinging pain in my left leg and another in my left shoulder, and I fell. Then they were upon me . . ."

> > . . . with the blood of which is customary to placate gods of this sort.

An orange death goddess from the southeast holds intestines in her right hand, puts them to her mouth with her left.

> ". . . in a minute, and one of them put his knee on my back, while another hit me a clip with a club or a butt of a gun. I don't know which, as I had no time to think."

> > The bodies they hang in the sacred grove that adjoins the temple. This grove is so sacred . . .

A green death goddess comes from the southwest, a blood-filled skull in her left hand, stirring it with a scepter in her right, drinking and enjoying it.

> "All I knew was that I was being scalped; my hair was held tight. I felt a hot, red-hot, stinging sort of pain all

around the top of my head, as I thought the hair were
torn out . . ."

. . . in the eyes of the heathen that each and every
tree in it is considered holy because of the death
and putrefaction of the victims.

*A yellow-white death goddess comes from the northwest, tears off
the head of a corpse, holds its heart in her right hand . . .*

". . . it was too much; I couldn't stand it; I died
at least I thought I did. But my scalp was saved
just as it was being torn off."

Even dogs and horses hang there, along with men;
a Christian told me he had seen seventy-two bodies
suspended there promiscuously.

*. . . puts the corpse to her mouth with her left, eats and enjoys it.
A blue death goddess from the northeast tears the head off another
corpse, eats and enjoys it.*

"The boys at the wagon had seen me running; saw
the Indians and came on, thirteen of them, and
got up just in time to prevent the red devils
from finishing their work. The Indians, as well
as my friends, thought I was dead."

Furthermore, the songs customarily chanted
in a ritual of this kind are so manifold
and unseemly that . . .

*These eight death goddesses surround the five deities of reason
which also come to you.*

"But I came to again and my scalp was laid back
again. It was only half torn off as you will
see, and it is growing again nicely."

. . . it is better to keep silent about them.

*

the Bardo (the Himalayas
of the mind)
Hat Creek (north
of Fort Laramie) or
Uppsala (north
of Stockholm)
Mean Time
1876
11th century

the bloodlust of
three races three ages three places
drains
this day
upon the table of sacrifice: the High
Plains
the heart
out of the dust
chants
the rounds
(from the north)
of life
the black death goddess
wasicunpi
the frost giants
(meaning either
the "spirits of the north" or
the "white men")
dance
.

Day 14 Tuesday, July 4, 1876

American*, will*
do
"(as another name for human, now, the ameriman?"
[Kelly queasily queries
our common shore]
Amerigo, mapmaker whose work
we worked to fill in
(100 years or
so) the empty spaces, went
out of our way to
clear & farm, tame, people, invest
in—claims on our blood
going
home. From the 4 doorways
of the world, the wild beasts come
& they are ours, & we are
saved from the fearful ambuscades
of the Great Plains by the realization
we are them, & they are
illusions
drinking our blood, draining
our illusions of freedom
of movement.

From midnight till dawn, 100 anvil salutes &
Deadwood's first son (Revillo) born this day
to a reveille of aureal revelry.

The Lord of Death can fill your world
with terrifying deities. You will know them
by their appearance: glassy eyes, upper
teeth biting lower lip, hair tied
in a knot on top of the head, big-bellied,
and carrying your karmic record with them.
They shriek: "Kill! Kill!" You will know them
by their actions: eating brains, drinking
blood, tearing out hearts, tearing off heads.

Scenes where we seem either
lost in the jaws of a berserker beast
after a feast or
our own fangs & claws found
nuggatory as nuggets of fool's gold
in a forest of gory nightmares
49 days deep. . . .

Still the dream-stunned dawn
of our second century draws
(& quarters in the brain) up
the Liberty Pole—a proud
yellow bole topped
with a big ball of gilt:
Old Glory by jingo!
From a field of blue
its stars like soiled doves
have flown the coup. (All
Deadwood's proto-DAR have dyed &
sewn its red on white from their own
unmentionables amended
by monthly menses &
mundane pee stains.) Now
underway the declamation
of the Declaration & signing
the petition

"... for speedy and prompt action
in extinguishing the Indian
title to, and the opening
for settlement of the country
we are now occupying and
improving."

the New World Tree   Dead Wood   cross cut   saw   mandala   rings

the Aurora
Borealis
sings
the song of sacrifice

old Lord of
Death
dances
from the doorway of the North
upon each beat
a heart

.

"The crack of small arms, however, could be heard
from every quarter from the right and the left, from the front and . . ."

Day 15 **July 5, 1876 (A Leaf From the Old Man's Journal)**

What his heart would write:

In the iron plight of our holds
a plainsong for the New World's bound
together with our myth-fate long
as the longboat of our father's
father held on the cold scales
of the fishes-road to summer's
far plunder at Lyndisfarne.
(Those were the days
before we came across
the bloody rood of the Lord.)

From the fallen towers of Troy
to smokestacks gagging
the dragon, we've blundered & hacked
our way. (The ship-wrecked
dragon found in the deep
sleeping ground at Sutton Hoo
the same year the hooked
cross drags its burning
dragon's belly across
Europe.) We've gone so far
as to carve rootless runes
in white marble mosques
at Byzantium. Exiled
from love, to the west
we founded lawless lands
of ice & wine, floundered
in new worlds of gold &
pain. Saved by the crossing,
our blood turned cold
in each vein. We put on
the conqueror's mask &
called it good
as our old coat of arms.

Now we're modern. Civilization
stokes its engine. Our fate its freight
train across the plain, we zero in
on the last power point vanishing
on the horizon. Lost with the sun
we wander long for redgold
won in the grassroots
of these weary Black Hills
here for the taking. Our hearts'
wooden hulls 've grown hard
as Skallagrimsson's skull.
Dry-docked, we long to see
the whole world drown
its last, soul-scorching flames
out. From the first sweat
of the fearsome giant
Ymir, our bloodlines were born
of ice. How (praytell) we'll die
in fire is well known. The gap between
is a chaos of days &

desire. (The canteen is empty.) Dreams
of sailing into the arms
of fjords heaped with glitter
-tales of war fade away
with the blood-gorged sunset
over Deadwood Gulch. Still
a few flecks of placer
might catch the eye. That's all
we have to remember
our sun-shattered glory by.

What his pen would scratch:

Rocked out some dirt
in gulch. Prospects not good.

Day 16 July 6, 1876

"You got about as much chance as a one-leggéd Chinaman
at an ass-kicking party!"

roars Thorvald thru his red beard bristling
with swallow winds the yellow pines. From its nest
in the west, the spotted eagle takes to the thunderheads
& circles the speck of frost giants' hall.
In the first contest the feckless hag rassles
this blowhard out with ease down
to his knees.

"Jeezus Kee-ryst!" invokes he the up & coming deity
of the day to no avail.

He's no frosh, but would take up the mead cup at the drop
of an insult. In the second his draught drains naught
but three fingers deep.

"Well I'll be a son of a bitch!" spits Thorvald.

In the third the paw of the big gray tom is all
he can budge off the straw-fake floor of the huge hall.

"Well dog my cats!" he capitulates.

To old age, the North Sea, & the World Serpent—
one two three these contestants change
as he's informed of their true nature under
their veils. His lightning-rage prevails & picks up
his bully club to beat the B.S. from here

to holy cow country. But now
by some theurgic quirk this whole spoof
goes *Poof!* & gone
with nary a trace. Alone
upon a spacious & airy plain,
Bloodaxe stands as a speck
of an eagle jets off
across the blue abyss above.

Day 17 July 7, 1876

From an upstairs window in the Grand Central Hotel, a barrage
of shots (or swats down them damn horseflies) becomes the aural
mirage of hunting & pecking the brand spanking Remington
Wayland Smith down the hall had shipped all the way
from New York: a type writing machine. The ribbon's tread
by Tommy the Spider as Lucky Coyote composes
per verses aimed at pedigreed petticoats in the manner
of doggerel taking after Catullus:

> YOU SOLD YOUR HEART TO A LIMP-PRICKED DADDY
> FOR ROSES AND CRYSTAL AND EVEN A CADDY.
> YOU SUCK AND SUCK UP TO ALL HIS RICH STUFF
> BUT THEN NEED A PUTTER TO PUT UP YOUR MUFF.

Lucky's got balls
that feel
like they've been driven
halfway down
the fairway
& back. Not sandwich nor -man can he stand. Stud-fast
he drives his buckboard past her darkened cabin, curses
the catty bitch out all night with the dratted lout.

> O NEVER AGAIN TO STROKE YOUR TIGHT CUP!
> YOU POLISHED MY DRIVER AND MADE IT STAND UP.
> SO GO DOWN TO-NIGHT AS YOU TEND HIS CLUB BAR,
> REMEMBER MY MEMBER WE JUICED TO BEAT PAR.

Heart-cracked Coyote sends Ink Tommy to crawl thru her keyhole, hiss
his verses, build his web of words, watch her
squirm—her shorts
pissed.

Day 18 July 8, 1876

"Who *she* show? Wha' *she* chew?"

A she-goat among bucks
showing hershelf shamleshly [sic]
(mouth full o' um . . .)
under moonclit prickpine.
A mare deriding men
to kick the wild oats bucket.
Fuckette of all the gods
& worm-sucked clods of Deadwood.
(Lucky cusses again, lady
luckless of course.) Nicemaid
mutter confessor, she sheds
redgold tears wishing
her 'spectors leadpans clean. She wants
to salt their brainpans instead
with dreams of fresh young flesh. Freya

owns a wagon, covered
with boars' blood, drawn
by two cougars. It quarters
her business: herself.
Stake to stake (out).
Rake to rake (in).
Lust to dust. (Must
frigg it to nugget. Dig it?)
After dusk she dons
her feather dress for all
the one-shot wans.

"Jist Juan an' he's Don. Ho!
Ho! Ho! Who! Who! Who! Whoa
Nelly!"

comes caterwaulin'
from the yeller pines. (A horny owl
with a pussy face.) By her berth
she keeps a chair. A-rockin'

like a mother's cradle, another
kind of cathouse wagon stocked
with all the purr-bearing feline feel
Phatty from Dogtown could steal
rolls into Deadwood. Miles after moonset, Mars
sextile to Venus, backed by Parker's
"sextet of tomcats," Freya scats
a timely raga, enthralls the thralls
of her strumpet thighs which scrub
down her brush:

> "My sweetheart vowed she'd wait for me,
> Till I returned, but don't you see?
> She's married now, so I am told,
>
> Left her lousy miner,
> Left her lousy miner,
> Who looks for shining gold."

Her slave-putzed wagon is lead
("Although no natural lakes occur in the Black Hills . . .")
down to an alchemical pond where
one by one, their desire (polluted) bodies are drowned
in fire. Their clairvoyant eyes
in occultation turn
to gold, as the grave weight
of wet dreams
lies.

Day 19 July 9, 1876

From his quarters on the north end
of Deadwood Gulch (a 2 bit broken
-down hermit's hutch), Doc Mimer
jots in his day book—his mundane worry
of money sabbatically
restless:

> "I had now been in this unhappy island
> above 10 months; all possibility
> of deliverance from this condition
> seemed to be entirely taken
> from me; and I firmly believed
> that no humane shape had ever
> set foot upon that place."

He reads the news released
into his visions, suns or moons
before it happens, tree rings
even—the morbid odds. Flash
floods or forest fires he forecasts
for Deadwood. For each pilfering pilgrim
a gold watch ticks off the megrim
in Mimer's head, then
the obit's written
in blood on a skull when
the victim will be taken. All the while
the doctor makes the rounds
from his well to the ill
& back. Empathically
20/20, his eyes flood
for the frail girl & her doll
with angel hair will fry
in a house fire tonight or
the spouseless juiced-up souse found
passed out in a snowbank
Thanksgiving Day a score of years
hence will be too useless
to even care about (they'll say). Or

is he a man dreaming
he's a ghost or
is she a ghost
dreaming
she's a girl?

The doctor's given to visions
& becomes them
who must pass on
his compassion
to the next world.

"This morning Charley was not feeling
well. I had to go to Town alone
Heard a sermon but did not hear
the text   no one Seemed to
pay any attention   Two Auctions going on
at the Same time."

In the brook of some quidnunc's babble
Mimer sometimes finds himself
a round white stone
& a black hole
within
the round white stone.
(The round white stone
is the narrow gate between worlds
of ice & fire, here
& forever.) He falls & is gone
a thousand years before he returns
missing
but one word in the flow.
As from a deep sleep
he rises—a puff of steam
streaming from his mouth.
Though he can't quite recall
the light of the world
where he'd been, the spirit
of the dream is enough
to know
the white stone within.

Day 20 July 10, 1876

Showdown. High
noon. North
end of Main toward
Slaughter
Gulch. The whole
town lounges in
shirt-sleeves & vests.
The sun an iron
crown weights on
each head. South
end of the street
a box
on a tripod. "Hold
it!" Hands on
hips or arms
crossed. Eyes
wander & laughter
makes
faces & forms
take
shape on the plate
ghost-like.
The light eats
a bit
of each &
spirits it
away
in obscura.

There's no beginning
& two ends to each
street. Still
till the shot's
done they all
of a sudden make
like a motion picture in
technicolor till

the projector
runs out of its
film
which forms
each form
of life here in
Deadwood.

Photo courtesy of Centennial Archives, Deadwood Public Library

Day 21 July 11, 1876

"May we be spared
a long and painful passage-way
across the plains.
In Jesus' name
we pray, Amen."
was the last word
many settlers heard
before setting out
for the land of the dead.
Certainly
it is written
by the mirror-luster himself
General George Armstrong Custer:

> "Sometimes the mirage has been the cause
> of frightful suffering and death
> by its deceptive appearance." Once there

upon the Great American Desert, the prairie
schooners in single file look like a string
of pearls. (Note the Castle Creek shot
Illingworth took on the '74 expedition
of the Black Hills.) From a distance
the whole nation of attacking Sioux
might really be a half dozen or so
slaughtered buffalo at point blank.
Waterholes turn out to be dust
devils. Ghost dancers' clothes
at sunrise evaporate as
the Will-o-the-Wisp would. Northern Lights
burn in columns of blood, purple
prose or shattered bullets
of yellow ore.

Know that life is unreal and
death is also unreal...

Deadwood & the medicine man's "bright red stick that was alive"
exist side by side. Upon the Great American Desert, the eyes
of the sun & the sunflower, visions & nightmares, peyote
buttons & glass beads, crossed paths (red & black) echo
the illusions of the Great American Desert.
The allusions to the Great American Desert
elude the truth of the matter of conquest
with the ol' "Give 'em hell!" spirit
of the West:

"It was gradually discerned that the Great American Desert
did not exist, that it had no abiding place, but that within
its supposed limits and instead of what had been regarded
as a sterile and unfruitful tract of land incapable of
sustaining either man or beast. . ."

(The Sioux here at least
since the year 1776.)

". . . there existed the fairest and richest portion
of the natural domain, blessed
with a climate pure, bracing and healthful . . ."

"When I look back now from this high hill
of my old age, I can still see the butchered
women and children lying heaped and scattered
along the crooked gulch as plain as when
I saw them with eyes still young. And I can see
that something else died there in the bloody mud,
and was buried in the blizzard. A people's dream
died there. It was a beautiful dream." (Black Elk's
red scene as yet to come
to pass.)

Know the couple in sexual union
and your other sights and sounds
are unreal illusions. They are
like dreams, mirages, echoes,
reflections; they are nonexistent.
So why seek them? Why fear them?

A LOG OF DEADWOOD

They all arise from within yourself.
Know, too, that even your own
consciousness is unreal, illusory . . .

My Life On the Planes or

Bury My Heart At Wounded Need

If you are to be born
on a western continent, you will see
a lake with horses grazing
at the shore. Do not enter
there now. There is wealth
and abundance, but religion is weak . . .
If you are to be born
a wandering spirit, you will see
barren deserts, desolate plains . . .

Day 22 July 12, 1876 (A Leaf From the Old Man's Journal)

Just as I fell
into the dark mouth
of the giant's daughter
Hel, bibliomantically
my *Germania* had fallen
open to the passage:

> "They do not reckon
> time by days, as we do, but
> by nights. All their engagements
> and appointments are made
> on this system. Night is regarded
> as ushering in the day." Hear

the nightmare: the noose around my neck made
of strands of whatnot—the noise
of a moving bobcat, the roots
of Bear Butte, sinews of that bear, the beard
of a woman, breath of a rainbow
trout & spit of a raven—round my neck

& shambling naked in the oak grove biting
the dust rolling unable to stand being pushed
into dark cracks rock & water the wattles
of a hurdle bear down in the bog my bugger's butt &
gawk at *what*?

I am my own murderer
lurking in bur oak & lupine.
I am my own victim
hung in my name, up, in the branches
of my bloodlines' fate burning
tracts of evergreen black. Earthquakes
tidal waves & hurricanes thunder over
the High Plains, merge into one
din: *Waste him! Waste him! Waste him!* &

I wake . . . (or do we wake only
as the dream is realized
for what it is: but a dream
dead to the world & longing
to be born) into the twilight
shades of lead-gray. The sun smolders:
a red ember in the west—its ashes
blown into my shack by the fierce winds
of karma. Before my bleary eyes
the Aurora Borealis flies. Never
to rest, day to day, my dreams
of the north sleep-walk
the world over.

Day 23 · July 13, 1876

In the parlor of the Progressive Hall, the portly
Wayland W. Smith whittling
away his day dreams
of a steam-driven flying machine
rising from the sun-crusted dust
off a Gold St. runway of someday
big-time Deadwood City. Somewhat bored
he cusses a lowly pillbug crawling
across the arabesque rug imported
from Persia (via St. Louie). Grinning & grunting
down on one knee, he
impales it with the point
of his stick.

Ho! Ho! Ho!
Ha! Ha! Ha! [read the broken newsprint
ad for the establishment]

All you thirsty mortals who want
a good drink, smoke, or a lively
time, remember that

Ed (Bull) Durham, (Handsome) Jack Gray [one day to run
& Madam Fleecy Fleck the Wasp Mine #2]

Have opened their new house on
Main Street Deadwood City
which will be known as . . .

Wayland drifts off
in reverent reverie
of what gold the science faction
of the future holds
in store: "A pinch
of dust
for a drink
of the elixir

vitae—or am I
just
dreaming this up?"

[one of the pioneers
of '76 later known
by the name 'Sooners']

Day 24 July 14, 1876

"Over beer the bird   of forgetfulness broods
  And steals the minds of men . . ."

Hang-
    (Tomorrow
     is another
     would-be
     dead-weight.
     Some days are   Diamonds
     better   (the ace of).
     off left
     otherwise
     unsaid
     & gone.
     Last night is.)
                over.
     Lucky the joker
     blacks out
     a night
     here, there
     shuffles
     it back
     into his pack
     of cards: days
     minus
     three aces.
     Hearts.
     Clubs.
     Spades.

"Over   forgetfulness broods
  And   the   men . . ."

Hanging in the oak grove, the mob
gone home, blackbirds flock
& perch on their shoulders, peck
their necks till . . .

Dead fall.

Blood drunk.

Night.

O holy.

No grave.

Nothing is.

Day 25 July 15, 1876

Mid-day / mid-afterlife span / mid-quarter
of fire in the balance.   With a torrid
nonchalance, the sun alone drops
its spectral order over the dead
& the undead alike.

Over the limestone plateau, thundering herds
of wild flowers bend against & shake
tender heads with the winds
both Yes & No. Wending away
thru Quaker aspen & paper
birch, yellow pine & white
spruce draped with old
man's beard, the source of Cold
Springs Creek in his ear
ululating hymnally
the spaced-out anomie
of linear time, Marcus Alias
is lost in the dense *wood* . . .

utterly senseless
woode
vehement   woo   raving
ode   rash   reckless
violence   wyrd   wild   furious   irascible
void   would   fierce   insane
L. *vátès* seer   Wodan   Of a dog or other beast, rabid
poet   OE. *wód*= OHG. *wuot*   (in
passionate   AS. Woden   od   *ferwuot*   ferocious
pain   Wotan   raging, frantic)
ON. *ódr*   G. *Wut*   rage   frenzy
poetry   chant   Goth. *wôd, wops*   possessed
Odinn   Teut. *wód-*, OE. *wóp*
Odin   intoxicated   song, sound
O'Din   Icel. *othr*   W. *gwawd*   song of praise, excited
OIr. *fáith*   poet   Othin   or inspired
From the mutilated stem
are OE. *wéde*   mad

wéden as in
Wedenonfa'
ague &
Widdendream
a state
of mental disturbance
demonium
delirium
a fit
a furor
animi
within

. . . the wood of his days ever
since the last night of spring
whispered a disembodied voice:

All alone, without friends
and loved ones near, alone
but for my innermost thoughts . . .

Across the Island of Despair, headed
for the Lost Mining District, Question Marc quotes
someone to himself [who
that very second himself is
stumbling thru the steamy jungles
of Java] (in translation
of course):

'I is someone else.'

"All have their balderdash alibi
for this *bright day*. Even me: I
is somewhere else, oddly doctored
by Mimer thru tomorrow. Or else
you could say I'm really doxied
by proxy by Freeley all night
at the Gem in Deadwood, dreaming
the place me's at or the face he had
before we was born. I am
something else: a motherless child

of the granddaddy river, the boy gone wild
west to outlandish adventure
in Injun Territory. . . ."

("I searched for the cassava root, which
the Indians in all that climate make
their bread of, but could find none.")

"Or cutting fodder
back, I'm Everyguise—
bald-faced son of a one
-eyed Jackov who'll
who-who even harder
than a Bardo Owl
over my dead body!
O Great & Terrible
Spear-shaker, you're gonna cry
96 tears!"

As the blinding eye passes on
somewhere else, a new dark will reign
regardless of innocence or
the omens Alias dreams on
his own
end: namely, the fatal
-istically fixed chain
of events which
link his life
& death with the brink
of world break-down
is known
by the father & the son
alone.

"I slept unquiet, dreamed always
frightful dreams, and often started out
of my sleep in the night: in the day
great troubles overwhelmed my mind, and
in the night I dreamed often
of killing the savages . . ."

Day 26 July 16, 1876

A specimen day
the most man alive
in the land notes
blithely in his sun & mudbath
the slow, well-balanced
          mating
in the wind of the two
crimson dragonflies over
Timber Creek just outside
Camden. The cottonwoods'
seed-balls drift off
to all the States . . .

"What deepening twilight—scum floating atop the waters
Who are they as bats and night-dogs askant in the capital?"

Grant in the White House
drinking himself
bug-juice dumb & granting
no more rations for the "red devils"
till they cede their deeded right

to the Black Hills. Eidólons
drifting like dust motes down
Whitewood & Deadwood cañons would
look in vain & blind faith
for fragments of gilt scattered
by the sun.

Corruption & filth in the War Dept. &
maggots in the brain
of the old glory-monger—the news
of whose defeat which stunned these States
like a sledge to the skull
of a slaughterhouse steer

red-shifts the Christian Doppler effect weeks after the fact:

"Injun talk is very Strong   Report Says
Custer is killed that Crook
is licked and that we are likely
to have a tussel here in Dead Wood
and that we are Sure to catch it
if we go out"

The good Graybeard walks back to his shack
& the stars seem more remote & farther
apart. They chant their seed-syllables deep
into the houses of night, deep
off the far end of the blood's spectrum.

Day 27 July 17, 1876

Mud out front the Bucket o' Blood
as a mass squashed around the stage
just in from Cheyenne bearing
the longed-for mail.
James Butler Hickok writes
his "own darling Wife" as
Martha Canary flutters
her lashes over icteric eyes
mocking some coquette. The wary
Doc Mimer watches the play
of light & shade on the barroom floor
form the acts of War Bonnet Creek
south in the Sandhills:

> In black velvet vaquero costume
> (silver lace & buttons slashed
> with crimson & gold, white
> sombrero plumed & pinned up
> on one side) Buffalo Bill Cody
> faces down the Cheyenne
> brave Yellow Hand, blonde
> scalp dangling
> from his belt, his balls
> guarded by a stained breech-bird made
> from the Bar-Stangled Spanner. . . .

Wild Bill orders the house a round
of redeye, proposes a toast in memoriam
the Little Big Horn "massacre."

> Red & white ride
> up a blue streak—trade
> shots—Yellow Hand's horse drops
> the second Bill's hits
> a gopher's hole—now both
> afoot Cody plugs him
> in the gut—twists

the blade of a Bowie deep
in his fist-shaped heart that sighs
one last death-breath
before he flies. . . .

Calamity Jane howls muddy blurter
as her body's taken by a foker-paced sharp
in a hand of jive-starred cud.

"Jerking off the war bonnet I scientifically
scalped him in about 5 seconds," remarked
the Honorable Will to bait the yellow press.
A line he would muster time after place under
one proscenium after another: "The first
scalp for Custer!"

Disgusted by both scenes, the good doctor
heads home—the blood of the good Indian
slurred in his vision mixed up
by too many deafening rounds of
"Here's mud in yer eye!"

Day 28 July 18, 1876

In the waters of night
she bathes. The moon swells
as milky light flows
over her breasts. Nipples
stiffen to sweet beads
in the chill mountain air.
Her cinnamon skin sparkles. Puddles
of shadows & Minnekahta mist
droplets cling to thighs &
round bottom. Ringlets
on her firm mound perfumed
with musk, murmurs
& sighs drift down the river
of her hair. A raven's wing
in the wind floats south
with sounds of the elk flute.

The sheriff rubs his eyes at the edge
of the water. He dreams her:
Woo-O-Pay, the star-fallen woman
he longs to enter. Charging
the body eidetic
of this peaceful deity, he's chased
by nimbus fleece burning up
the north. It grabs his gut, punches out
his daylights. Luminescence
consumes his haunches, scorches
his testy essence. Tongues flicker
blue flames to drink his blood
dry, lick the limp muscles
off his skeleton. He topples
like a house of cards
to a heap of bones. A skull &
a pair of cobalt eyes stare
as she dives in the river, emerges
a white buffalo. On the glassy surface
of the water she walks his dream

upstream, her hooves leaving a trail
of ice-moons glowing. Slowly
drifting toward him, they melt
in the whispering current
of night, whispering again
& again his name: "You're insane,
Tyrone Tyrane. You're insane . . ."
                                        Sheriff Tyrane bursts
upon the blinding plain
of day as if he were dropped
from the air. He's whole again.
It's barren & cold. (Is it
the windstorm of his spirit
expiring? Or the maimed roaring
from the phlegm-green north
of the Great Bear he hears?)
From beyond the time-frozen rim
of the fimbul winter, the wrathful
polar deity Coup-Was-Zee
rears up the dizzy height
of his holy butte. A squall
glazes his white fur full
of Hel's lice. He glistens
with ice-needles, sharpens
his claws on the ledges
of Devil's Tower. Legerdemain
is his domain. His legend
is Legion. Paws upraised
he rushes headlong thru ponderosa
pines for the man strong-armed
by his logged karma. As he strangles
the trigger, Tyrane's firearm drips
hot lead in his hand. He shrieks
& flees the hailstorm
in his heart. Whirlwinds of sleet
knot up the thought
in his brain. Bear claws swipe
at his back. He hears: scratching
branches against glass, mashing
of his skull, collapsing into itself

of matter, thunder cracking
limbs. As static legs turn
to sticky rubber, the sun shatters
into flying slivers. His liver's
ripped out & eaten. His heart gives
way like a dike. A wall
of boiling blood gushes
across the fallen plain
of this day, flooding & staining
his vision red. He thrashes
in his own ocean, drowns
                                        in the drop
to his bed: a dead birch
crashed to the porch, shards
of panes scattered
across sheets, rain
beating on his face—
the salt taste of blood
the oldest law.

Day 29 July 19, 1876 (A Leaf From the Old Man's Journal)

The time it takes
to draw back a bow/to
let the arrow go
I change
my mind
& my body
follows: feathers
fletching the shaft in order
to keep direction
straight. Shape-shifter
they call me
& I must come
& be
them: Ball
of Fire, great
Head or terrible
Beast, lovely
Lady, spotted
Eagle or rattle
Snake.
          Time is a weight
          on my mind (wind
          time, wolf
          time.) Places
          exchange
races. What was
hovering on the horizon
a mass of thunderheads or
the nest of Thunder Beings turns
into a thicket of evergreen
at close range. The 'spectors'
quixotic jackpots are lead
somewhere over the rainbow into
what was
the late Lakota holy land.
The yellow brick road crosses
the cracked & run-down inter-state

the buffalo used
to migrate: the Milky Way
to the spirit world, the red road.
Even an "ally" changes to
a "little adder"
(Lakota: Sioux).
Like theirs, the lines
in my face, blood or my race,
palms or lives, seem
reflected in the rocks'
chaos like dream-clouds worn
by wind or time. White-water creeks
dammed at dusk into little lakes
wind up mist at wolf-day's
first lap. What one
mistakes in the distance
as something hard
to climb & conquer drifts
off, dissipates: droplets
of water. Yellow owl's clover
or pea-sized hailstones, gods
& goddesses of earth & air
take lovers from one
another, mix
spit & mettle, honey & blood
of the wisest
truce-born giant. At the heart
of the highest
spruce-worn peak
east of the Rockies (the white-hides name
"Harney") my eyes seek
the magic mead otherwise
known as "mouth-gold."
As a lone rattlesnake I see
poetry dripping from the horny lips
of She-Who's-Hot-Under
-the-Rocks. I come to
make it with & take off
as a spotted eagle. Fast
in my beak this lap-liquor or

first verse-honey's held. Spilled
poetaster's piss &
bard's breath commingle
(like sperm & ovum) our firm
democratic vistas with
a womb-dream only the most select
& sacred of shamans can
incant.

Day 30 July 20, 1876

Near the highway the High One's
crows lie as bushwhackers
for mule deer, prairie dogs or
jackalope. In a bullwhacker's wagon
ox-heart Bloodaxe lugs
his blue-frocked freight:
the pig-tailed whippersnapper
in ruby slippers. Miss Gale hugs
her black terrier as they gaze
upon the bloody tonsure
of the mail carrier—letters
scattered white about
his skull. At break-neck day up
Almira Gulch, the Sioux pursue.

"Toto, I've a feeling we're not
in Kansas anymore."

Thorvald shakes his head. No
time to check his luckless pard
Chuck Nolin. The wild & woolly

~~West~~

sous rature: a few signs
of fleece, fur, buckskin, bones, blond hair &
a gold filling now & then—
the gap [Hollo remarks] in Memory
& Thought. The twin blackbirds
over the earth extend fairly
O'Din's central nervous system.
Sympathetic, he's most concerned
for the bird he can't recall.

"Don't travel away, stay home if y' can,
Stay away from that city, they call it Cheyenne,
For the ol' Sitting Bulls and Comanche Bills,
They will lift up yer hair
in the Dreary Black Hills."

From the sacred sage's & shortgrass prairies'
poppies to the ever-popular green
shades of Emerald City, there's no place
like home, where the heartwood is.

> "O I'm a-goin' home—
> Bullwhackin' for t' spurn,
> I ain't got a nickel
> An' I don't give a durn.
> 'Cause when I meet a purdy gal
> You bet I will or try,
> I'll whack her with my ox-bow,
> Root, hog, or die."

Day 31 July 21, 1876

At the World's Fair in Chicago, 1893—
.44s drawn, outrider for Colorado
Charley (his Pioneer Pony
Express to Cheyenne), unshy
Freya's pistoleer protegee
Miss Canary re. the query
on the nature (ontological) of her question
-able character:

"Say you lop-eared, slab
-sided, dirty neck, you
knock-kneed, pigeon
-toed, splay-foot
son of a
skunk, I'll show ya
who I am. I'm the real
Calamity Jane, General Crook's
scout, a howlin'
coyote from Bitter Creek—
th' further up
ya go, th' bitterer
it gits, an' I'm from th' head
end. Now you apologize
'fore I shoot th' damned
toes off yer feet!"

She'll wander the rest of her days, dazed
this way. That she believes
she is she echoes
down the midway all the way
back to Deadwood, resounding. Here
her howl now, off these cañon walls, echoes
there, off those, from the Fair
& back. And forth. As if she were
a pair
of prairie wolves caught
in separate traps—a year

here, a year there, where
they're howling to each other
                                        to be
                                                            set free.

Day 32 July 22, 1876

A play within a play
of light & shades
of gray, fitts
of sadness, wits
of bizdom, a capital
pea unfounded
under what
in a nutshell.

"*Real* bodies on a *real* stage!"

A little night magic.

the upright piano prof professed
unproven.

Illusion of the stage.
Illusion of the world
of the stage.

"The Languishe [sic] troupe will make
their first appearance in their
mammoth pavilion theater, and give
the first dramatic rendition ever
["The Banker's Daughter"] witnessed
in western Dakota this evening."

Rendition: surrendering
to the elements
of the acts, the scenes, the flow
of events—the willing
suspension of disbelief, giving
in to the illusion.
Into the elements
of suspension, an element
of surprise—the theater
in the round, the world:

"It rained during the performance,
the roof leaked, and Main Street
became a quagmire." A part

of the play, the stage, the plains
perform
these sleights for our entertainment—
horror or delight.

. . . being apparent yet non-existent
in reality, like a form produced
by a magician. That is called
the pure
illusory form.

In the drama, the deluge
on Main Street: the delusion
of Deadwood.

Indeed, all these are like dreams
like hallucinations,
like echoes,
like the cities
of the Odor-eaters,
like mirage,
like mirrored forms,
like phantasmagoria,
like the moon
seen in the water—not real even
for a moment.
In truth, they are
unreal.
They are
false.

Like the moon painted
on a backdrop, reflected
in the real pool
in the deluded mind.

Day 33 July 23, 1876

Sun enters the Lion
(the heart)
on its way south
(thru the mouth)
is most what it is
(a torch)
consuming
(runes blazing within)
the blood on its way
out
.

Year the of rat.

Full moon of the red
chokecherries.

Dog days.

"Scarcity of Game Elk meat and venison
so plentiful in the Hills a few months
ago. . . Buffalo no longer come near
the Hills in numbers we doubt whether
another one will be seen within
a hundred miles."

The rat gnaws at
the gut of the man
in the moon:
who's hungry.

Beans, white (lb.)	$0.18
Bacon (side)	0.22
Salt (lb.)	0.10–0.15
Beefsteak (lb.)	0.15–0.20
Sugar (lb.)	0.27
Coal oil (gal.)	1.25–1.50

Sun Dance starts
the moon
the cherries turn.

Gall bladder of cow:
cure for insanity.
Gall bladder of bear:
liver infection.
Hedgehog skin (from the head)
dipsomania & piles.
Tiger bones mixed with harts-horn
& shell of terrapin:
debility & rheumatism.
Acorns:
dropsy & epileptic fits.
Fish bones:
cancer.
Powdered rhinoceros horn:
small pox fever.
Dried maggots:
jim-jam fever of dysentery.
Dried caterpillar:
hoarse throat.
Dried rats:
restores hair.

"Full details of the butchery
of Gen. Custer and his forces
and of the disastrous fight
of Gen. Reno in the same
engagement, reached us by stage
and pony express last . . ."

Rain In the Face blasts
Yellow Hair thru the head, cuts
out the heart, impales
it on a stick, dances
round & round, eats &
hears the singing
of birds as speech.

"Cattle die, and kinsmen die,
And so one dies oneself;
One thing I know that never dies,
The fame of a dead man's deeds."

Hours of the dragon:
7–9 a.m.
Hours of the dog:
7–9 p.m.

The Strong Heart Society
". . . killed the dogs
of prominent families
and when the dog was shot
they shouted and shook
their rattles. It strengthened
a man's heart to have his dog
killed and not show
anger. The woman singed
the dogs, cooked them, and
took them to one
of the Strong Heart lodges.
There they all sang
and danced, and the dogs
were part of the feast."

If loved ones make offerings or sacrifice animals in your name and you become angry, you will be born at once in hell.

"There is but one sentiment
on the Indian question here—
the hostile Sioux
should be exterminated, and
white men engaged in trading
ammunition to them
should be hung
wherever found."

"The unicorn ends up coldcuts;
the dragon as meat pie."

"This is a good day
to die," the red son said
of the goods—his heart
hard as a cherry pit.

". . . the cherries were pounded
to a pulp, pits and all
on stone mortars, and
after being shaped
into small cakes, were
laid out to dry in
the sun."

Day 34 July 24, 1876

As the sun sunk to sputter
its burning sulphur, the last breath
of day sucked cloud-scuds
eastward into the gaping mouth
of evening. In the yen-she den
under Deadwood's main drag, a black ball
in the golden bowl dreams
an orange moon inhaling
the lit matchstick.

Tunnels & running
water, footfalls & roar
of a hundred languages
foreign & lost all
at once
in time for ever
in ears of stone.

The ax in his hand, the man
with his head hacked off . . .
"He fought the gods & lost." thought
Yellow Doll, her body screaming
thru a rock wall. A thick
black mat of hair on his chest, his nipples
(blood-spattered & crusted) blink
& stare back a pair
of blue eyes, half-human.
"Hsing-t'ien! Hsing-t'ien!" hisses
the hair lip of his navel.
Her white silk waist coat, flowing
sleeves dyed with April
-pink petals, tatters
like a flag in a wind
tunnel. From the ceiling
of the kerosene-lit cave, her spirit
afloat on waves of fear watches
her doll-body on the floor

broken like china. The ax dices
her heart pumping
all over, her
insides pulled out &
stuffed down the hole
his lost head left.

She cannot leave.
She cannot die.
She is already
dead.

High above her men in white robes lower
her casket. Firecrackers brass gongs & cymbals
split the incensed air. They've left
a basket of fruit, a black roast pig,
a white snake, a red cock. At the gravesite
they've scattered red squares
of paper like bits of skin—each one
pierced with a pin-prick
the ax-man must pass thru
to get to her
celestial home the golden dragon
of dream guards.

He is already dead.
They are living
the realm between lives.
He has come to
Deadwood due to
what he has
done. They are already
trying to re-do
their undoings.
He has not
learned. They are
already living.

Day 35 July 25, 1876

A day in the life

(Dead

Wood Gulch) between

lives

Day 36 July 26, 1876 (A Leaf From the Old Man's Journal)

Good or bad
it says it
in the Book
of the It: IT
chooses
it. An amoeba or the crab
nebula looks back out
the frag of glass tacked
to the wall of my shack.
The mirror-spirits are growing
stronger & will
no longer merely mimic in
total exactness.
Not I AM nor Legion but
IT
is fate. To be
chosen as a candidate
for the clap or the sacred
thunder of madness.
The "backward"
shaman (the Lakota
heyoka) dreams
it in
lightning or
the Lights flitting & flaring
out
of the north reflect
IT. No word
on the other side
of the glass ever
sees IT
to its end.
ITs sign
is when
my form is
not found in the looking
glass at all &

it is all
lost in IT.

IT is a boiling river
    running beneath my eyes.
IT is a white-hot ember
    the world & all
    its objects burn with.
IT is ". . . a seething pot
    and the face thereof
    is toward the north."
IT is the weary hordes of heat waves wavering
    off the searing plain of Hel.
IT is a whirlwind pinwheel
    within a wheel within.
IT is the golden cottonwood leaves
    of the New World Tree—each one
    a little mirror fluttering
    hot flashes under
    the sun.
IT is the molten sunlight itself
    scribbling a mystick script
    on the wind-wrinkled sea.
IT is a war of corposants
    pulsating patterns
    of coruscating colors.
IT is a phosphorus jellyfish afloat
    in the aqueous humor whispering
    the swish & splash of chaos.
IT is the dazzling squadrons of zigzagging
    squid—dizzy spasms of squiggles swimming
    thru the haze of the head & the fuzz
    of what was.
IT is a synaesthetic fizz & buzz
    at the crossbone base of the skull known
    as tintinnabulations of tinnitus.
IT is a yeasty, lustrous froth
    of balloons & bubbles & bombs bursting
    in the eyes & the morning-after red beer.
IT is a curtain of blood & a streamer of dream

swirling thru the ever-nimble fingers
of a nimbus wind.
IT is a spectral maelstrom of atomized rainbows.
IT is a veil of shades restlessly rustling adrift
with gossamer ghosts across a field
of vision & profusion of fission.
IT is a filmy sheen of undulating hushes.
IT is a shimmering chimera of shattered prisms
scattered to the solar winds
by the Great Bear.
IT is the sands of random time
& space suspended midair in the ether kingdom
of unearthly power & empyrean glory forever.
IT is the effulgent phantoms
of wickedly writhing pornagraphees.
IT is the scintillating titillations
of dated bodied blazing, astrologically
fated as a log of dead wood.
IT is their passion-flushed illusions of flesh fed
to the wrathful deities who
chew them up & spit them out
in a blizzard of confetti.
IT is the sky-gurry of lances & blurry shields.
IT is the unreal reeling of all magnetic fields.
IT is the evanescent aura of the north
Death dances across the heavens.
IT is the Aurora Borealis roaring
across this page like the hangman's horse.
IT is she whom I call
my very own
mount White Breath.
IT is all
the rage
& the whole story
my race
will recount
for 49 days within
each wayward soul sown
on this blank plain
of the slain.

Day 37 July 27, 1876

"Away, I'm bound away,
'cross the wide Missouri."

Thorvald Bloodaxe, wood butcher,
sluice worker, bullwhacker, would-be
homesteader, recalls (with pathos overshadowing
eros) his old world. He sees the sun-up
cast shadows over his shoulders
like trout. Out of the cold waves
of night over the plains they flop
around his campfire's white hissing
embers. He'll take great pains
to forget. Across the muddy river
of morning, his family members
gather in the patriarch's parlor
in black. He waves & waves, calls
out but—Damnit!—he's too far gone
on the other side to hear
or be heard. Deaf fire
is the nature of his word.
A film of ash floats
like a jellyfish under the surface
of his face. In his palm
he holds a live coal
cold as an ice cube. Unfleshed

out, he'll wander the day &
the rest of his days, seeking
some dark woman to enter, to come
& be no more & blissfully drift
on womb-waves nine moons before
he's washed (a new world
unto himself) ashore
to carry on the mark
of his blood-acts within.

Day 38 July 28, 1876

You will see visions

of couples'

copulations

Visions will come.

"Come-on-stick-it-in-an'
fuck-me-oh-shit-fuck-hard
harder-come-on-quick . . ."

If birth is to be obtained over a heap of impurities, a sensation that it is sweet-smelling will attract one toward that impure mass, and birth will be obtained thereby.

He-goes-down-on-her-cracks
her-lips-spew-hot-juice-over
his-lips-tongue-her-clit-sucking
it-down-&-rub-&-kiss-both
tits-stiff-nipples-scratching
his-ass-screws-her-mouth-come
both-at-the-same-time-lapping-it
up . . .

At the same time, emit
thy gift waves upon the womb
which thou art entering, into
a celestial mansion.

Her-ass-unabashed-in-the-air
he-humps-her-from-behind-his
whelp-whimpering-itch-after
each-grunted-thrust . . .

You will see visions

of copulations'

couples.

Couples will come &

you will come to

choose one

womb, the perfect

visions thereof.

Her-crablegs-cocked-over-his
shoulders-hung-balls-slap-her
butt-slick-frigg-finger-up
his-furry-bung-hole-squirming
eel-like-she-licks-his-nips-&
pubes-quiver-mucus-quick . . .

. . . of human beings, enter
into the great mansions of
precious metals and into
the delightful gardens.

Glans-big-as-a-plum-&-cum
a-cup-of-quicksilver-wet
vulva-velvet-soft-her
peach-juicy-&-bitten-red
fleshy-at-the-pit . . .

You will see couples

of visions'

copulations.

Copulations will come.

"Oh-god-I'm-coming-I'm-coming
don't-stop-go-fuck-me-ah
fuck-me-oh-god
damn-fuck-me-please
me-oh-yes-now-oh
oh!-oh!-oh!-ooooh!"

O nobly born, if thou art not able to rid thyself of attraction and repulsion, and know not the art of choosing the womb-door, whichever of the above visions may appear, call upon the Primordial Trinity and take refuge therein.

Copulation.

Couples.

Visions.

Of a mother (born-again): perfect.

Day 39 July 29, 1876

Tong boss & heap
big man in the joss
house, Coolee Q. keeps
the Secret
of the Golden Flower
to himself. He lotus-postures himself
in the quiet room. Bones
of dry wood. Heart
of cooled ashes. His blood
turns to pure milk. White jade
steps lead from his golden house. Outside
the air is hot & thick
with hoppers. He is quiet
between the moon & the sun
(the eyes) & the breath
of the four winds.

Balanced
as well:
fate & will
ming & hsing
water & fire
K'an & Li
☵ ☲

mate in the field
a square inch big in the middle
of the square foot house (the head).
It's entered thru the red hall
(the mouth) which comes (lead)
at last to the golden
pill, the fertile lapis: elixir
of life that flowers
thru the circulation of light
in the heavenly heart while
the earthly heart's covered
with gray owl wings (the lungs).

Balanced
as well:
anima & animus
yin & yang
eros & psyche
life & logos

lie in the field
of the dark house, the heat
mixing & melting the dark
slag of seed-water & spirit
-fire to conceive
in the crucible (the spirit-womb):
the golden embryo out of which
the spirit-son grows.

Between the moon & the sun
& Coolee's soul-stilled orbs:
the Pole Star
the Third Eye
the Tai Chi
fixed
in the flux, the Way, the Tao, the Aurora B.

"But worldly people who do not understand
the secret words of the *Book of the Elixir
of Life* have misunderstood the yellow
and white: they have taken it as a means
of making gold out of stones. Is that
not foolish?"

As he watches the petals
of the sun unfold, sympathetically
Coolee's head blooms. For a living
he washes the masses
of goldbugs' duds, fixes
their grub. Above Deadwood
the air is hot & thick
with hungers. Bristling
thru hordes of fat hoppers, maggots
quicken in that
all too human heat.

Day 40 July 30, 1876

"I feel my days
are numbered. My sun
is sinking fast. . . ."
Wild Bill
deals the sourdough
California Joe
a straight flush rising
with the stacked passing
of the catty calico queen
of hearts, Freya. The maya
of kerosene lamps up & down
Deadwood Cañon throws a dance
of shadows in the nightmare
quagmire on Main St. As a leit
-motif of death wafts forth
& back, a quavering fire runs
the hurdy-gurdy gauntlet
amuck.

"Goodnight ladies, goodnight ladies,
Goodnight ladies, we're going
to leave you now."

Up in the air: another life
a certain perfume triggers
& you're there! Her come-on
showdown, that go-gone
hold-up number waved
down a long way
off, an error of gold
ago.

"Somewhere in the Black minin' Hills o' Dakota
There lived a young boy named Rocky Rac-o-o-o-o-n . . ."

Back & forth, from one bar
to a nether, baritone
or tenor, Melodeon
or guitar, tambourine time

at the Green Front, timbre
& melody tangle: lusters lost
in the jangle. The whir
& rattle, the dizzying swizzle
of roulette wheels' steel
balls clack & battle
the odds. Cockeyed
& crapulous, you bet
on the glittering beat
fortune wills at random
to the devil's kingdom
or God's.

> "Of all the comrades that I had
> There's none that's left t' boast;
> I'm left alone in misery
> Like some poor wanderin' ghost."

Butt to the back bar
of the Gem, Lucky quips
with the gutless boxherder
Johnny Burns (his yes-man)
of poker chips. The former
clips his nails to cache in
his Coca bottle, build his boat.
Warped, Coyote sees himself
a latter-day Noah.

> "An' as I pass from town t' town
> They call me the rambling sign—
> 'There goes Tom Moore, a bummer shore,
> Of the days of '49.'"

Beyond feeling, the sheriff rides
his cayuse in, pocks the ceiling
with his six-gun, drinks to his self
-abuse. Listing like he's hit
an iceberg, (off the log) he falls
to the sawdust seabed.

"In the days of old, in the days of gold,
  How oftimes I repine—
For the days of old when we dug up gold
  In the days of '49."

High on White Rocks that echo
the low-down whoop-up
of the Beast With Two Backs (nee
Deadwood) Doc Mimer ponders
the minor pitfalls of his etude
of solitude:

"... yet to enclose my self among the hills
and woods, in the center
of the island, is to anticipate
my bondage ..."

"For my heart is filled with the days of yore,
  An' oftimes I repine—
For the days of old, for the days of gold,
  For the days of '49."

Day 41 July 31, 1876

The Mississippi man Marcus Alias, newcomer
to the bummers of the Sioux Territory, begins
with a bad dream of some gallery: below
he sees the ceremony over one two three
closed coffins—himself, Tom, & Joe.

Freya's so afraid
she makes all the elements
swear: metals, rocks, & woods
would dare not harm our dear
Marcus. After that the 'spectors draw
buffalo bullseyes on his chest
for target practice. Their bullets all rebound
as if he sports a death-proof vest.
At last a blind bro lead
by pro-con Lucky (hand held steady)
tries his aim. His gun loaded
with six cold rounds forged
from the Golden Bough fires &
Marcus (alas) falls dead.

All the elements, but one
Hel-cat Freeley forgot.
The metal most on the minds
of fools finds the pure heart
of O'Din's long lost son.
In his ghost-white ear Farley whispers
what remains to this day
moot as the third root. With a leaden tear
the All-Father comes to place
upon the pyre the old ring
the sun mirrors: the gold one they call
"the Dropper." After the casket
on a prairie schooner's set
afire, the north wind casts
his ashes over the vessel: a *vas,* hermetic
melting pot filled with the dross
of its gilded dream. In the wake

L. Coyote incognito would flee Deadwood
pronto. Down the snakeback Bad
thru Missouri mud to the slurry
of old Miss, this trout-face treads
out where the mouth spits
its inland silt
                    to the salt sea.

Day 42 **August 1, 1876 (The Judgement)**

white stone black stone
                    black stone
                    black stone

                  "Well *I* say
                   I didn't do
                   nothing!"
                              (His day in court.)
                   black stone
white stone black stone

On the scales: the weight
of Coyote's fate (extradited yesterday
by the way by
Corporal White) fails
to balance.
                    This underdog appears
                    in the mirror: in one flash fucking
                    his daughter White Breath (the shape
                    -shifty Lucky in the form of a mare
                    once bore), the next his flesh
                    switches to a witch-like crone. She alone
                    tears up ice in his eyes while
                    the rest of the town drowns
                    in mourning for Marcus, who lives
                    no more—alias
                    the Shining One, the golden son
                    of the god (the Old Man had become
                    in the 'spectors' eyes) in the west
                    has set, as darkness grows
                    rotten in the fate of Deadwood.

"I'm not *all* bad. At least
I gave fire
to folks," Lucky boasts.

No good. Outside a mob of Black Hillers
is itching to lynch. The mad triad
of O'Din (paired with Tyrane), Thorvald, & Freya
makes up the Board of Death—the illusive form
of city government which rules as one
lord over no-man's land between
lives . . .

black stone
black stone
black stone
no more.

With crowd grumblings & cries
of *Hang him! Hang him! Hang him!*, the mass
storms the jail, drags out
Coyote by his scruffy tail, hacks off
here & there a pound or two
of flesh—stew meat that grows back
greased lightning. They tie up this tough
cur with a rope wound from the stuff
of his wolf-gutted son. (Junior's moniker:
Big Nosed George.) They hang
overhead a rattler spitting
stinging juice at Lucky's eyes—batty
& bloodshot. His judgement
(or lack of it) fixes him for good (or
at least till twilight
of the last dog day).

Tommy the Spider spins
a web of curse drops
of ink stick to
like dew. An hourglass to go
before Coyote's got balls
(black stones) enough to bust
free to do
lewd battle with all
the white hats
Deadwood can muster.

The price of the binding (the book
thrown at Lucky): the Law's right hand
missing. Sheriff Tyrane's star
catches fire from the redgold
of the sun, catches Hel
in its five tin fingers. His fist
pounds in the pit of Coyote's gut
like a heart attacking
                              its rabid blood.

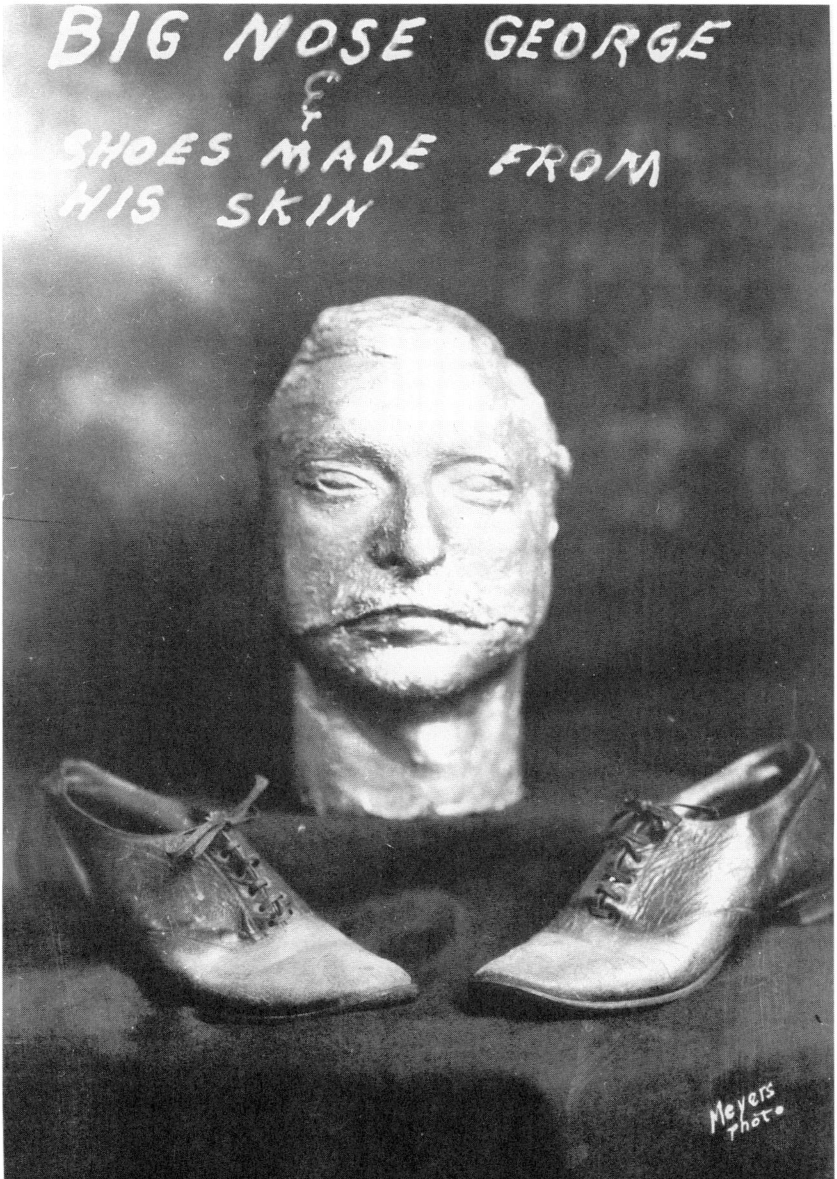

Death mask of Big Nosed George

Day 43 **August 2, 1876**

Gung ho & hard on
high noon, Coolee Q. likes to lope [12 p.m.]
with Yellow Doll (borne again)
astraddle his lap. Bucking
up in the tantrick saddle down
on Deadwood creekbed, she rides—rushing
no pearls of rebirth off
her mountain oyster but
those that come out the head
the spirit-son grows
(ecstatick) from. Over
her shoulder in a field
of flux, a buzz

see-saws their balanced blissing: he sees
a bone-white wrist sticking
out of the grass, stumbles over
the statick form of Will
Cowan—a voided
whiskey flask stinking
by his side, horseflies
rigorously kissing
the mortised zero of his mouth.

*

In a trance, bound but
on his way, wrapped up
in a buffalo blanket tied
with rawhide thongs, Coyote lying still
& dumb on the cold dirt floor
of the jail (rattler hanging
from the rafter) breaks
wind—phew! A spotted eagle flaps up
out of his butt. Out of his mind
the *yuwipi* bird perched
on the window sill takes off

to do his bidding. "I'll meet yer ten
an' raise y' ten," bluffs Captain Massie
to the new tin-starred Deputy
W.W. Smith. Round the poker table
Marshal Hickok & Sheriff Tyrane
clockwise kill time in Mann's Saloon
Number 10—drinking & playing the day
away. Mugs of Gold Nugget beer slide
the length of the bar. Beards flecked
with bullcakes & sawdust, pards argue
their claimstakes. Freya sidles up
to beef-breath Thorvald, combs
her fingers thru the red curls
on his broad chest. In the corner
O'Din stews over a brew, his slouch hat
down over his right eye, the other
a dead moon rolling in the bitter humor
of his still-mourning head. Across the room

Doc Mimer checks his pocket watch. [3 p.m.]
Smith sits at 6, Massie at 9, the Sheriff at noon
& Wild Bill at 3 o'clock—his back
to the flapping doors on which
the eagle has landed. A black
widow crawls across Hickok's hand
of aces & eights. Out of the beak
spits the phantom of this mellerdramer:
Crook Nosed Jack cracks
his pistol-whipped manhood—

"Damn you, take *that!*

Blam! As the rear
of Hickok's head's blown
into his snout, the bird's up &
the assassin's out
the door & rassled down
by the meat market before
shell-shocked Freya can say:

"Wild Bill's been shot!
My ol' Bill's dead!"

After a trial factitious as
fool's gold, the killer called McCall
was lead (the noose around his neck)
when the news broke: "Injuns [6 p.m.]
surround Deadwood! All able-bodied
citizens with firearms and mounts
asked to render assistance."
Wild Bill's killer (whose brother he says
Will Bill killed) was left with the end
of the rope in his hand, standing
in the street where the miners' court found him
free of guilt to go: his sense
of vengeance going back
to the days men stuck
to their guns, to their blood.

* *

"Just at Sundown a Greaser come in
with an Indian Head This caped the climax
Wild Bill and evry thing else was
thrown in the Shade. The Greaser was
Surrounded and carried through Town when [9 p.m.]
they reached the upper end of Town there was fuly
two Thousand men hooping and yelling Such a Sight
is Seldom Seen anywhere"

In Deadwood a young redskin's head
wise as the doctor's, an old lore
sleep-talking from its lips, spirits
of a tongue coming from afar, whips
a medicine up on the north winds
of war:

"someone
somewhere
is speaking

from the north
a sacred-stone nation
is speaking
you will hear
someone
somewhere
speaking"
(the translation):

"The head was Strung up on a pole
put up at auction carried around
to the places of Busyness and the people
asked to give the killer one
or five dollars just as he liked
a horrid looking thing to make
So much fuss about"

The White Stone Men
the spirit-spheres
the mystery-stones:

"all these
move with a purpose
a sacred-stone nation
moves with a purpose"

The spirits of the dead
dwell within
the white stones
moving
toward Dead Wood.
The Lights of the north
feed their torches
moving
with a purpose
toward Dead Wood—
in the sky
in the eye
moving
moving

somewhere
someone
is speaking
from the north
a sacred-stone nation
is speaking:

"I am Grandfather Rock.
I am standing
still.
I am everywhere.
I am the sacred-stone nation.
I am Grandfather Rock.

My brother's name is
Sky.
His secret name is
That-Which-Moves-Moves
(*Takuskanskan*).
Brother Sky is moving
the Lights of the stones
in the night.
The Lights of the north
dwell within
the sacred-stone nation
in the night.
The round stones are moving
in the night.
The *yuwipi* stones are moving
in the night.
The black night is moving
the white stones round
& round.
Round & round
the stones are moving.
Round & round
the stars are moving.
Round & round
the Lights of the stones
are moving.

A Log of Deadwood

Round & round
the Lights of the north
are moving.
Round & round
the stars of the spirit-people
are moving.
Round & round
the people gather
everywhere.
Round & round
the spirit-people gather
the sacred stones.
Round & round
me the people
gather.

I am Grandfather Rock.
I am the Sacred Peak
at the center of the world.
I am the Sacred Peak
of the Tree of the people
at the center of the world.
I am the oldest Peak
in the Black Hills
at the center of the world.
Upon the oldest Peak
of the Tree of the spirit-people
at the center of the world
lives the Star-Which-Never-Moves.
He is standing
still.
I am Grandfather Rock.

I am the center.
I am the oldest night.
I am the stars moving.
I am the Peak standing.
I am the stones moving.
I am the heart
of the Black Hills.
I am the heart
of the Lights
of the north
moving.
Still
I am the eye.
I am the eye of the heart
I am the eye of the heart of the Sacred.
I am the eye of the heart of the Sacred Tree.
I am the eye of the heart of the Sacred Tree of the spirit.
I am the eye of the heart of the Sacred Tree of the spirit-people.
I am moving.
I am standing.
Still
I am Grandfather Rock."

* * *

Blasting off
their pages in a whirlwind
of stinging gnats, the last words
the Old Man would write
(the goldbug idiom per diem)
for ages takes flight
from the chewed-up leaves
of the New World Tree
of Deadwood:

"It is getting dangerous here
to be healthy. A man is liable
to be Shot here at any time by [12 a.m.]
Some Drunken Desperado. and
it is not very Safe to go
out but we have decided to go

to morrow   any thing is better
than Staying here   all we have to do
is to Start and fight
our way through if necessary
we have good Guns   none better
plenty of munitions
of war   no very good feeling
for Mr. Lo any how
So here goes"

Across the sky celestial warriors
unbraid their hair, paint up
for war, say their prayers.
The Gathers of the Slain make
their journeys over the centuries
from the other side
of the globe—their shields
glistening in far fields
of stars. The Borealis flashes
searchlights on red souls
in ambushes. Hearts smolder &
the time is near.

Day 44 August 3, 1876

White Breath the night mare
rearing up her fury turned
into the New World Tree
fasting Farley hung on, wounded
by his own spear: himself
to himself given. His spurs
were whirling galaxies
dug deathly deep in
her wheezing flanks.
Wanting wisdom now, he
sees the runes &
reaches down thru bloody mist
& haunting hate to
seize them up
with a white-knuckled fist.
Shrieking & ruddy
he swoons & breaches
the might-buckled wall
of fate growing between
White Breath & Death, knowing
it soon will fall.

> "Then I began to flourish and wisdom flowered.
> I grew well and joy flowed through my growth.
> Each word led me on to another word,
> Each deed to another deed . . ."

His steed's blood-rite roots
in the old, bit
by bitter cold
of the Hel-serpent beneath
the doctor's well.
The Pole Star's her stud
-stuck Third Eye like white
mud upon her forehead.
A spotted eagle sits
on her right ear & shits.

Scurrying like a squirrel
from high to low, O'Din's soul
makes the rounds around
her rings that grow
no more. The fate of the world's
read in the swirls
in her grain, the knots
in her brain. Stippled
with milk & honeydew
her nipples are nipped
in the buds
by a mountain goat
& a whitetail buck.
In lamb's duds
Coyote-cum-Wolf prowls
a quick greenback.
"A new order
of the ages is born . . ."
(Again: wind time, wolf
time.) In the peering eye perched
on the apex of the pyramid
the beholder herself appears
tender.
Her heart's a reactor.
It melts down
to Chinatown or
the Japanese mourning (beginning
with the A
-bomb dump) of the world.
Mushrooming by the hour
Z (as in Ground Zero) she
is a real ash
upon the tongue rooted
in the blank rune
of Deadwood.
Her syndrome's
Rome's. Her empire
is fire.
She's a rocking horse
with wings.

A rocket ship
with oars.
In a dead heat
her eight legs blur.
At a dead end
she strides stern & stately
as four pallbearers. (Instead
'spectors she three
roots of the Tree
burning.) O'Din rides her
bareback
to Death
& back. Back
from Death
to this day
O'Din rides her
backwards: always
sees Death
eye to eye.

(Aye, to this day
Bloodaxe blindly trolls:
"O Dakota land, sweet Dakota land,
On thy burning soil I stand . . .")

Horse to Tree.
Tree to Horse.
Back & forth
head to hoof
White Breath by
giving birth
to the Sky
& the Earth
is living
proof the ax
-is mundi
is the source
of Deadwood.
Ax in hand
(the handle
aflame) old
Lord of Death—

bored with gold
black with shame—
come tear's day
will fight &
wound the wood
her heart fires.

Day 45 **August 4, 1876 (Black Mass)**

El C.'s
squared white
buffalo blanket

-y-

blank rune

Day 46 August 5, 1876

The gold-crocked witch
of Freya's mud-old bloodlines once
rose from her ashes
thrice & kept on
mining from the veins
of Deadwood's 'spectors the spoils
of the first war.

> "Brothers will fight   and fell each other
> And sisters' sons will   frigg their sick mothers;
> Hard it is on earth   with mighty whoredom . . ."

of the last war.
The fire-water witch
under the wane moon turns
to hoar frost
any body (heavenly or . . .)
which spurns her. Buggers
herself with a poker
-hot pistol of gold.
Sucks off sky gods
& spits bullets
into babies' bellies.
Out of the bog & cold mist
of the Will-o-the-Wisp:

> "Dark grows the sun   and in summer soon
> Come mighty storms: would you yet know more?"

The gold-crapped witch
of the West wickedly known
as Volva rose, cracked
Bloodaxe jokes & lip-sync.-ed
sybil songs—the sear fire
of her lust-sown vulva pierced
by the seer ring
of gold. Bold red

of the first war
of gold. Old blood
of the last war
foretold
by the first ice
& gold
of the last fire
& gold

of the otter shape-shifter
Lucky black stones
to death.
He heaps its hide
with ransom glitter.
The ring on its whisker
sings
to death
(in the echo chamber)
the life of the wearer.

In quest of what
the "giant's words"
of Mimer mean, a miner hears
the wyrd sisters' blues
bounce off the cañon walls &
lose the beat someplace
downstream. He sees blood
in his placer, a prairie wolf on the other
shore. (Would you yet know more?) It
is too late. His fate (like O'Din's)
thickens in his chest. The heat
brings killer bees & flies
to feast. The crow of Memory
carries off a nugget in its beak—
heart-shaped & bloody. The eclipsed
ring of the sun sets
a shining example in the West.

Day 47 **August 6, 1876 (The Garden of the North)**

The first man & woman: Ask
& Embla, ash & elm, on the shore—

driftwood? Or. . . Dead
to the touch &
O'Din gave the word, their souls &
the Silent One who'd outlive
the final fire (the wand of
prophecy to be given) gave
them understanding, though little
is remembered of him
now but his name (. . . . . .)

Flesh of the worldly tree: ash.

". . . fossils. The oldest one
recognized belonging to the order
is a leaf impression identified
as *Fraxinus* from the early Cretaceous
beds of Greenland (of about
80,000,000 years ago)."

The winged seed: the ashen keys seek
to lock the twining
helix, her locks falling
upon the likes (love) of
her breasts—a cascade
of color. The golden flutter
leaves the match
plenty to feed it. Heat

in the beginning given
as a blessing flames
in the garden, consumes
the kitchen midden. Sticks

the trickster Lucky rubs
together, ash into elm
into ashes, fucking
into oblivion a kingdom to come
out the other side of
Ragnarok—the maidenhead with
all the answers
                miraculously
intact.

Day 48 **August 7, 1876 (Riffling the Deck of Days)**

In-bourne on the back of the eight-leggéd horse
intact.

From the Eastern Realm, over the deep
a shining example in the West.

From the Realm of the South, land
blank rune

From the Western Realm, the fire
her heart fires.

From the Northern Realm, the frost giants come
the time is near.

From the 4 directions of the heart (together
its rabid blood.

from the throat the knowledge leaves
to the salt sea.

From the headwaters on down
For the days of '49."

Thorvald Bloodaxe & Wayland Smith were
all too human heat.

On her day Freya freely
Of a mother (born-again): perfect.

Drunk & barefoot up
of his blood-acts within.

"I will lift up mine eyes unto the hills, from whence cometh
of the slain.

A white death goddess from the east holds a corpse in the right hand
lives

Ameri*can, will*
already living.

What his heart would write:
the sun."

"You got about as much chance as a one-leggéd Chinaman
in the deluded mind.

From an upstairs window in the Grand Central Hotel, a barrage
set free.

"Who *she* show? Wha' *she* chew?"
Root, hog, or die."

From his quarters on the north end
incant.

Showdown. High
the oldest law.

"May we be spared
"Here's mud in yer eye!"

Just as I fell
off the far end of the blood's spectrum.

In the parlor of the Progressive Hall, the portly
of killing the savages . . ."

"Over beer the bird   of forgetfulness broods
Nothing is.

Mid-day/mid-afterlife span/mid-quarter
dreaming this up?"   by the name 'Sooners']

A specimen day
the world over.

Mud out front the Bucket o' Blood
barren deserts, desolate plains . . .

In the waters of night
Deadwood.

The time it takes
the white stone within.

Near the highway the High One's
lies.

At the World's Fair in Chicago, 1893—
pissed.

A play within a play
across the blue abyss above.

Sun enters the Lion
in gulch. Prospects not good.

As the sun sunk to sputter
from every quarter from the right and the left, from the front and . . ."

A day in the life
dance

Good or bad
together; and every mountain and island were moved . . ."

"Away, I'm bound away,
of all the boys."

You will see visions
all *obiter dicta.*

Tong boss & heap
inalienable reservation.

"I feel my days
over the mirror of its pages.

The Mississippi man Marcus Alias, newcomer
leaves   from the throat the knowledge

white stone black stone
make.

Gung ho & hard on
rising red, but on the run.

White Breath the night mare
He's the riding boy!"

El C.'s
sore.

The gold-crocked witch
fades away.

The first man & woman: Ask
wayward Deadwood burns with.

Day 49 August 8, 1876

T – 3

The day breaks
cold. The time is now.
(Ax time, sword time . . .)
Over Deadwood the sun
in a black mood rises
blue & full
of blood & phlegm
& falls
into the bruised arms
of storm clouds. The gold-combed
cock crows. *Ragna rök,* the 'fate
of the gods' or
rökkr, the 'twilight'
dawns.

> *There will be a gray twilight-like light, both by day and by night, and at all times.*

(Wind time, wolf time . . .) Again
the old chaos has come. Upon the horizon
the World Serpent churns up waves
on the inland ocean. Over the earth
it spits its burning poison.
With breath heavy as a furnace
in Hel, the prairie
wolf opens its mouth
wide as the sky &
downs the sun.

Casting no shadow, Corporal White
has been pacing the width of the rainbow
-ribbed bridge all night.
Back & forth at the end
of the spectral span (a life
of years or days

of death): two severed heads piked
(the medicine man & the doctor) jabber
between the keen-eared White's walk—
their chants intense as last rites.

"Yum Yata Yuwipi Wazi Tate Takuskanskan Hununpa . . ."
"Whirling move moves north to weeping bare wind
thru stone snow pines . . ."
So many lives
(the Lord of Death has undone, life
after life) crowd the archway
of the flaming bridge over
the river of daggers!
Under a dead weight
it twists & torques, strains &
breaks into icicle bits
smashed & scattered
on the rocks below.
Like a waking 'spector's dream
of gold, it melts away.

White sees rising
on the horizon of opposition
like a blood-sunk quartered moon hung
on a nail: a quirk-ark
of ghost-claws plowing
prairie swells. His cock
sowing serpents of fire, green
with hunger, helmsman Lucky gnashes
his fangs like thunder.
Tongues of forked lightning
lick the bloated sails
of the north-bound longboat built
with coffin nails. It makes its way, wave
to wave like a drunken coyote fleeing
trunk to trunk in a forest
of flames. White raises his horn
& sounds with all his might
the warning of the last morning
resounding from Pole to Pole to split

the dome of the sky open
like an axed skull. A crack
in time. A black hole
in space. Back & forth between
the Poles. Between the sun & the Moon
of the Black Chokecherries. Set
between the eyes
of O'Din at the center
of the Sacred Peak, the one
ring that never dies: wedded
to the heartwood
of the New World
Tree at the center
of the Black Hills—
the Great Mystery
                    holy beyond
                              belief!

> ". . . a mini-black hole passing through
> the body of the Earth and out
> the ocean might well have set
> off earthquakes and should have
> initiated a tidal wave . . ."

From the 4 doorways of the world:

> *Snow, rain, darkness, fierce blasts*
> *of frost, and hallucinations of being*
> *pursued by many people likewise will come,*
> *and sounds of mountains crumbling down,*
> *and of fierce winds springing up,*
> *and of roaring fire,*
> *and of angry overflowing seas.*

Across the red plain flickering
blue flames like snow
blowing its bitter ghosts over
the expanse of the well frozen
in Hel, the dead & the undead alike
advance toward the last war

the world will ever know.
(Would you yet know more
of areal earth, mon
hypocrite amour?)

"Yippee-ai-ay, yippee-ai-oh,
ghost-riders in the sky."

T – 2

North becomes everywhere. The stars
whirl down from their stations.
Down the rimrock cañon the 'spectors
of Deadwood pour their flash flood—
a boiling river of quicksilver toiling
toward the Plain of Death to war
against the forces Coyote commands.
At the noon of this day's night
the moon oozes: a blood-eye
puffed up above the storm
of warriors writhing like fire
-breathing serpents. Locked tail
to jaw (the rune-scarred
carving in ancient wood) tells
the old god-rush fate

to its end. With ax-sweat
& daggers, Thorvald kills
the World Serpent, staggers back
nine paces & falls—a victim
of its venom. Tyrane faces off
Lucky, whose black gorge looms
the Law's final tunnel. The scourge
of dead wood, ash-swords hack
Freeley to bloody ribbons. Playing havoc,
the frost giants toss Mimer's head
back & forth as the prairie wolf
gets pricked by O'Din's spear.
Yet today's Urth is the fate

of the ages: the All-Father follows the sun
swallowed whole. White rages against Coyote—
but neither withstands the other.

From the northern quarter
the sacred-stone nation bashes
(like x-rays) the battle plain.

"... matter [as it passes into a black hole]
will, as its death cry, emit
x-rays."

The White Stone Men
hail the fallen hosts beyond
recognition:
Thorvald's forearm
Coyote's scrotum
Freya's thigh
Mimer's mouth
Tyrane's hand
White's ear &
the flash of O'Din's eye—all
appear on the smoking Plain
in one mound of ghost-flesh.
The Lord of Death looks on:
his Hel-bent ring
decks it in one round
wall of fire
after another, mounting
concentrick. With full *futhorc*
death spells: money bull/saddle thorn/mouth torch
on the wooden teeth
of White Breath, the eye
of the Sacred Peak sees
the flood of fire
climbing (day by hour
& year by ring)
toward the pure heart
-wood of the first spring.

In the vernal quarter
    the blinded black killer of O'Din's son sees
    the blue wisdom
    of Reflection.
In the summer quarter
    the white buffalo woman Woo-O-Pay sees
    the yellow wisdom
    of Equality.
In the autumn quarter
    the yellow holy man Coolee sees
    the red wisdom
    of Clear Sight.
In the winter quarter
    the unread Marcus sees
    the green wisdom
    of Perfected Action &
at the center
    the Divine Father-Mother
    Life & Life-Giver
    living on morning
    dew as the sole source
    of the new race sees
    the prism wisdom
    of Omnipresence.
    (Where the center is everywhere &
    the circumference . . .
    the round dance.)

Island in a sea of flames
toward the blank rune
of silence sucking light
sound into itself.
I-land in a sea of blames
crumbling rock rumbles
an atomic dance under.
Ai-land in a sea of shames
toward the center (time
-lapse) collapsing.
Aye-land in a sea of names
White Breath feeds

mystick seed-syllables.
Eye-land in a sea of fumes
ignites the Dionysus
spacecraft to "Lift off!"
into the night
                    of the last day.

T – 1

If you are to be born
a warring frost giant
you will see a great forest
or rings of fire
revolving
in opposite directions.

Upon the horizon look
for no lover to ride
in (in any form) thru the pyromania
hoopla to save your hide.

"I fell into a burnin' ring o' fire,
I went down, down, down,
An' the flames went higher . . ."

Upon the horizon look
no further. Upon your death
the outside world forever
saw you frozen upon the event
horizon like a shadow.

". . . if we could observe something dropping
down into a black hole, we would see
it move more and more slowly as it approaches
the Schwarzschild radius, creeping ever more
slowly until at the Schwarzschild radius
we would see it stop
                              dead."

Still you passed on
to this new circle, this black
shield, this charred disk
between lives. You are drawn
toward the Central Realm
of the Densely Packed
(singularity). Therein
images (drop by drop) meld
into smell. Sounds melt
into touch. Tastes fuse
into thought as matter
compacts at the center.
Degree by degree, inward
& upward (calorically) toward
Polaris, the 4 directions
reverse vectors & collide
like Armageddon's armies.
Imploding in the eye
of the heart of the New World
Tree, Ground Zero
mass & infinite
density: the golden Wood

OUT
flowing
flowing
flowing
holy
ring
around
the black hole
a
round
singing
.
roun
". . . whisper, secret council . . ."
singing
"A dark or mysterious saying . . ."
singing

"A form of speech; a language."
singing
". . . writing . . ."
singing
". . . a book, an epistle."
singing
". . . a runic letter, a . . ."
rune
flowing
"A watercourse."
flowing
"Course, onward movement, *esp*. of
the heavenly bodies; running (of
persons)."
flowing
". . . of blood."
flowing
runes
blood-runes
of gold
singing
in
the heart
of Dead Wood
flowing
OUT
the center
ring
singing
.
In the sky
the maelstrom trail
of boreal ashes
the spotted eagle
spirals
within
whirls
its burning
whorls
wheeling

inward toward
the golden Word
written
on the Emerald Tablet
within
.
Y(O)U
will seek
the center
of the bliss-instant
of conception.
WE
have heard
the Book of the Dead
Wood speak
the sentence
(dog or pig
ant or grub
calf or kid
lamb or man)
our twin
helixes spin.
Around
the Earth
axis
I AM
the round
dance till
time stands
still
the Pole
Star falls
to sound
our birth
chant's
white
hole

A Log of Deadwood

A
O(U)T
M

A Selected Bibliography

The Tibetan Book of the Dead, compiled and edited by W.Y. Evans-Wentz, Oxford University Press, London, 1980

The Tibetan Book of the Dead, translation by Frank MacHovec, The Peter Pauper Press, Mount Vernon, New York, 1972

The Tibetan Book of the Dead, translation and commentary by Francesca Fremantle and Chögyam Trungpa, Shambala, Boulder, 1975

The Secret of the Golden Flower, translation by Richard Wilhelm, A Harvest/HBJ Book, New York, 1962

The Poetic Edda, translation by Henry Adam Bellows, The American-Scandinavian Foundation, New York, 1968

The Sacred Pipe: Black Elk's Account of the Seven Rites of the Oglala Sioux, recorded and edited by Joseph Epes Brown, Penguin Books, New York, 1979

Asimov, Isaac, *The Collapsing Universe: The Story of Black Holes,* Pocket Books, New York, 1977

Custer, General George Armstrong, *My Life On the Plains,* A Citadel Pioneer Book, Secaucus, New Jersey, 1974

Dumézil, Georges, *Gods of the Ancient Northmen,* University of California Press, Berkeley, 1977

Froiland, Sven G., *Natural History of the Black Hills,* The Center For Western Studies, Sioux Falls, South Dakota, 1978

Jung, C.G., *Psychology and Alchemy,* translation by R.F.C. Hull, Bollingen Series XX, Princeton University Press, 1980

Kelly, Robert, *The Common Shore,* Black Sparrow Press, Los Angeles, 1969

Rimbaud, Arthur, *Illuminations,* translation by Louise Varèse, New Directions Books, New York, 1957

Tacitus, *The Agricola and the Germania,* translation by H. Mattingly, Penguin Books, New York, 1977

GARY DAVID grew up on the south shore of Lake Erie, and attended Kent State, the University of Kansas, and the University of Colorado. He has lived in New Orleans, San Francisco, Santa Fe, and for a dozen years in the Black Hills where he received a fellowship grant from the South Dakota Arts Council. David has worked as a furniture mover, hotel desk clerk, gandy dancer, country western guitar player, TV ad copywriter, college instructor, and Artist-in-Schools poet. His poems have appeared in a number of publications, including *As Far As I Can See: Contemporary Writing of the Middle Plains*, *The Greenfield Review*, *Haight Ashbury Literary Journal*, *Salthouse*, and are forthcoming in *The Redneck Review of Literature*. His first book, *The Possibilities of Blue Sky*, was published by Northland Press in 1989. He currently lives with his wife and daughter between the Badlands and the Black Hills.